Date: 3/23/22

MAX AXIOM AND THE SOCIETY OF SUPER SCIENTISTS

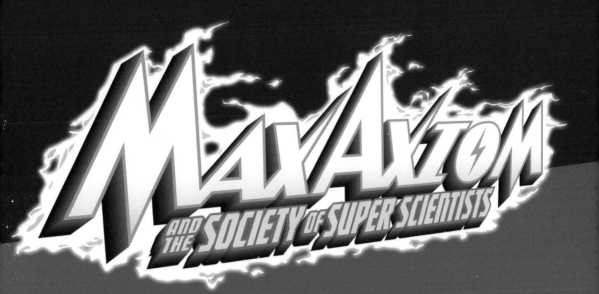

OCEAN PLASTICS PROBLEM

BY ELIZABETH PAGEL-HOGAN
ILLUSTRATED BY ERIK DOESCHER

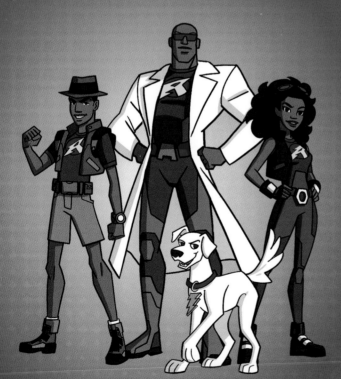

CAPSTONE PRESS
a capstone imprint

Published by Capstone Press, an imprint of Capstone.
1710 Roe Crest Drive
North Mankato, Minnesota 56003
capstonepub.com

Library of Congress Cataloging-in-Publication Data
Names: Pagel-Hogan, Elizabeth, author. | Doescher, Erik, illustrator.
Title: Ocean plastics problem : a Max Axiom super scientist adventure / by Elizabeth Pagel-Hogan ; illustrated by Erik Doescher.
Description: North Mankato, Minnesota : Capstone Press, [2022] | Series: Max Axiom and the society of super scientists | Includes bibliographical references and index. | Audience: Ages 8–11 | Audience: Grades 4–6
Identifiers: LCCN 2021012673 (print) | LCCN 2021012674 (ebook) | ISBN 9781663921758 (paperback) | ISBN 9781663907516 (hardcover) | ISBN 9781663907486 (ebook PDF) | ISBN 9781663907509 (kindle edition)
Subjects: LCSH: Plastic marine debris—Environmental aspects—Juvenile literature. | Plastic marine debris—Environmental aspects—Comic books, strips, etc.
Classification: LCC TD427.P62 P34 2022 (print) | LCC TD427.P62 (ebook) | DDC 363.738--dc23
LC record available at https://lccn.loc.gov/2021012673
LC ebook record available at https://lccn.loc.gov/2021012674

Summary: Plastic is everywhere . . . even in our oceans! But how did it get there, why does it matter, and what can we do about it? In this nonfiction graphic novel, Max Axiom and the Society of Super Scientists go on an exciting, fact-filled mission to find out.

Editorial Credits
Editors: Abby Huff and Aaron Sautter; Designer: Brann Garvey; Media Researcher: Svetlana Zhurkin; Production Specialist: Laura Manthe

All internet sites appearing in back matter were available and accurate when this book was sent to press.

Printed and bound in the United States of America. PO4270

TABLE OF CONTENTS

SECTION 1:
A BEACH EMERGENCY 6

SECTION 2:
PLASTIC IN THE OCEANS 12

SECTION 3:
FINDING SOLUTIONS 20

TAKE ACTION! 28
MORE PLASTIC FACTS 29
GLOSSARY 30
READ MORE 31
INTERNET SITES 31
INDEX 32

THE SOCIETY OF
SUPER SCIENTISTS

MAX AXIOM

After years of study, Max Axiom, the world's first Super Scientist, knew the mysteries of the universe were too vast for one person alone to uncover. So Max created the Society of Super Scientists! Using their superpowers and super-smarts, this talented group investigates today's most urgent scientific and environmental issues and learns about actions everyone can take to solve them.

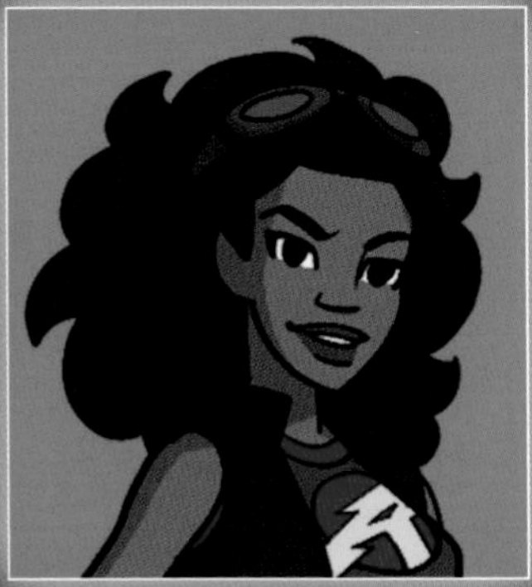

LIZZY AXIOM

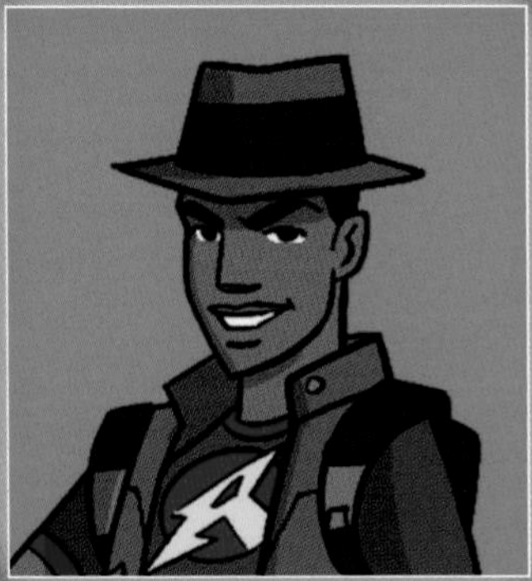

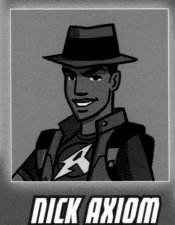

NICK AXIOM

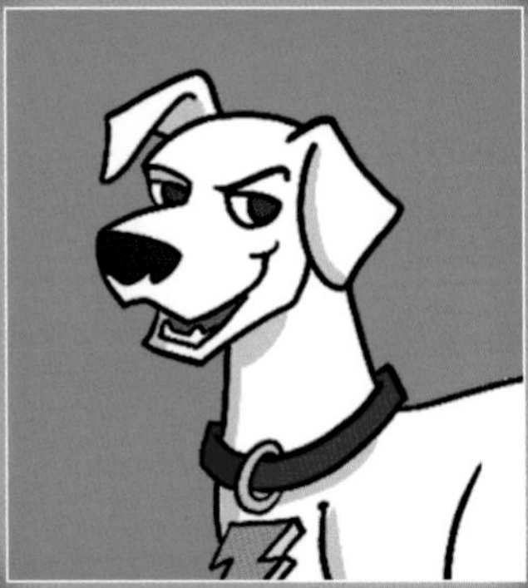

SPARK

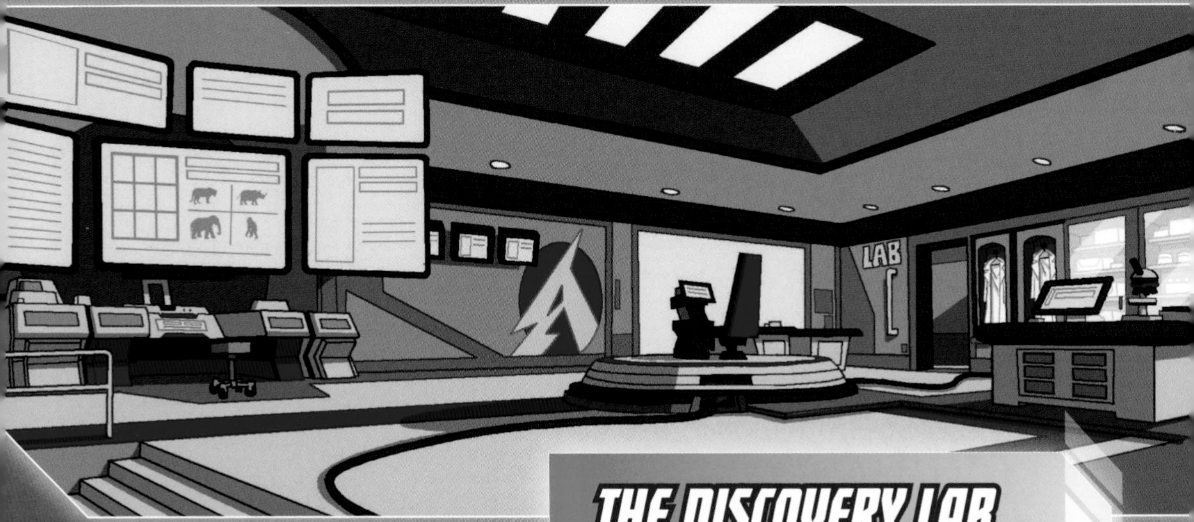
LAB

THE DISCOVERY LAB

Home of the Society of Super Scientists, this state-of-the-art lab houses advanced tools for cutting-edge research and radical scientific innovation. More importantly, it is a space for Super Scientists to collaborate and share knowledge as they work together to tackle any challenge.

SECTION 1: *A BEACH EMERGENCY*

As the Society of Super-Scientists answers an emergency call at the beach, they discover an even bigger problem. . . .

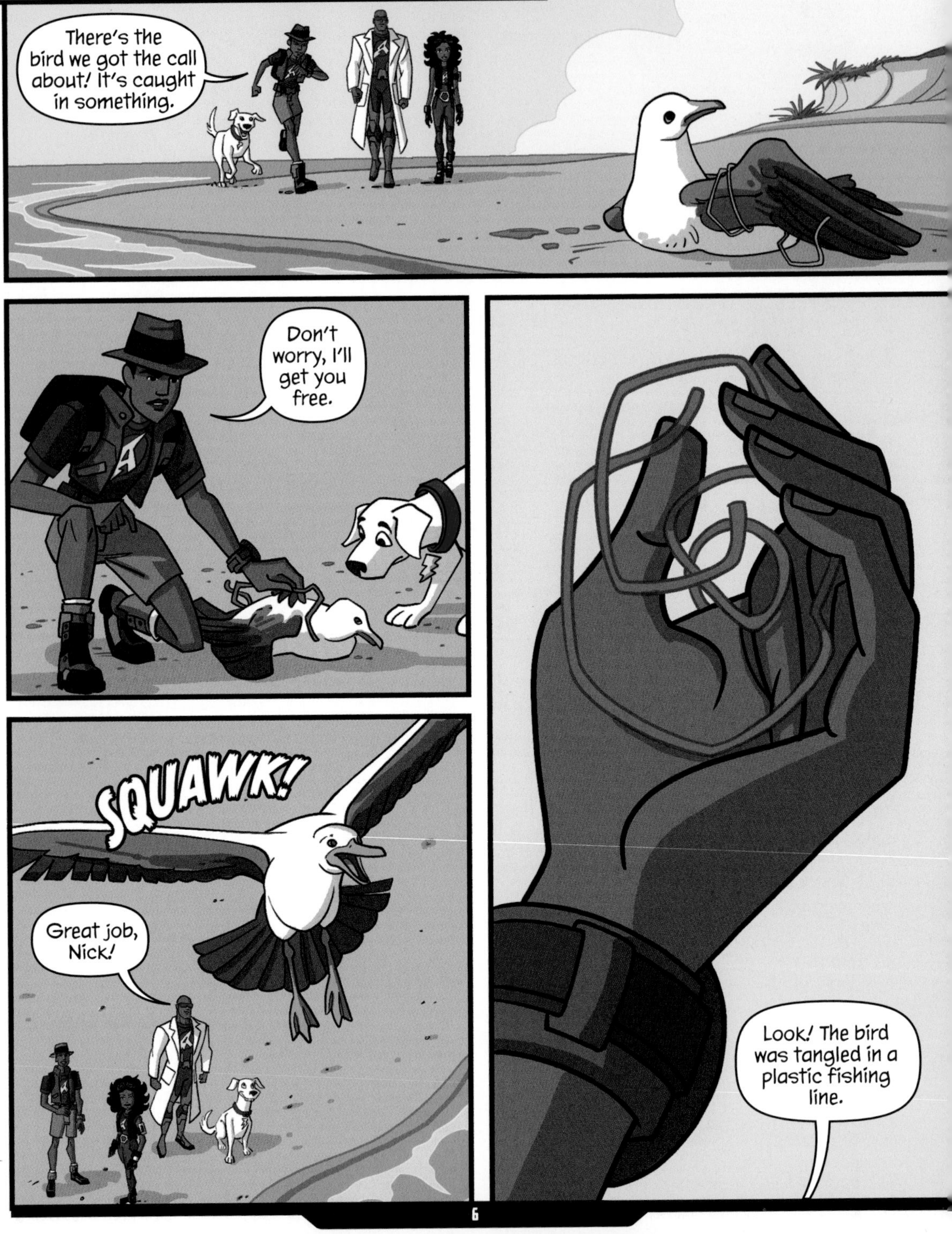
There's the bird we got the call about! It's caught in something.
Don't worry, I'll get you free.
SQUAWK!
Great job, Nick!
Look! The bird was tangled in a plastic fishing line.

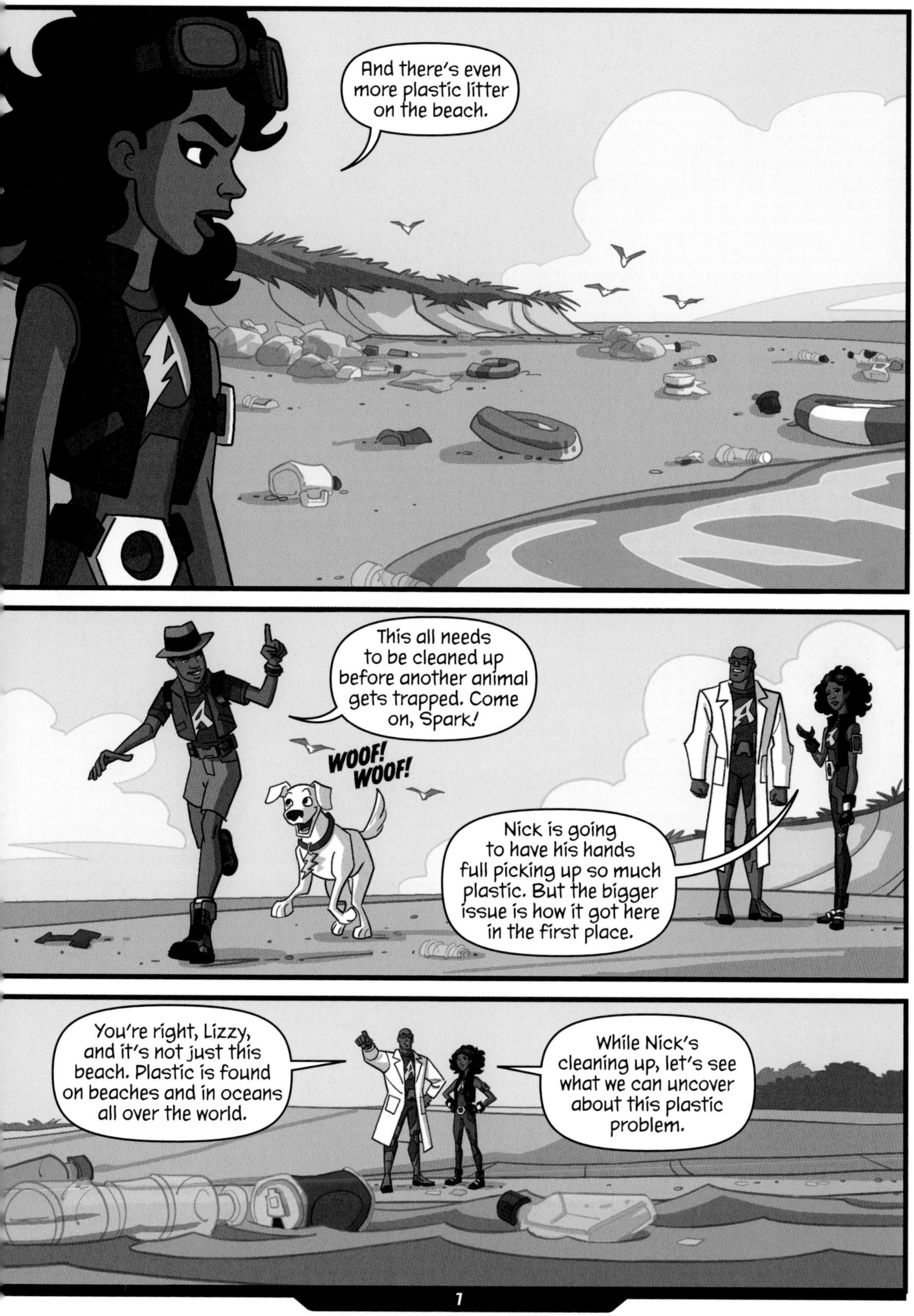
And there's even more plastic litter on the beach.
This all needs to be cleaned up before another animal gets trapped. Come on, Spark!
WOOF! WOOF!
Nick is going to have his hands full picking up so much plastic. But the bigger issue is how it got here in the first place.
You're right, Lizzy, and it's not just this beach. Plastic is found on beaches and in oceans all over the world.
While Nick's cleaning up, let's see what we can uncover about this plastic problem.

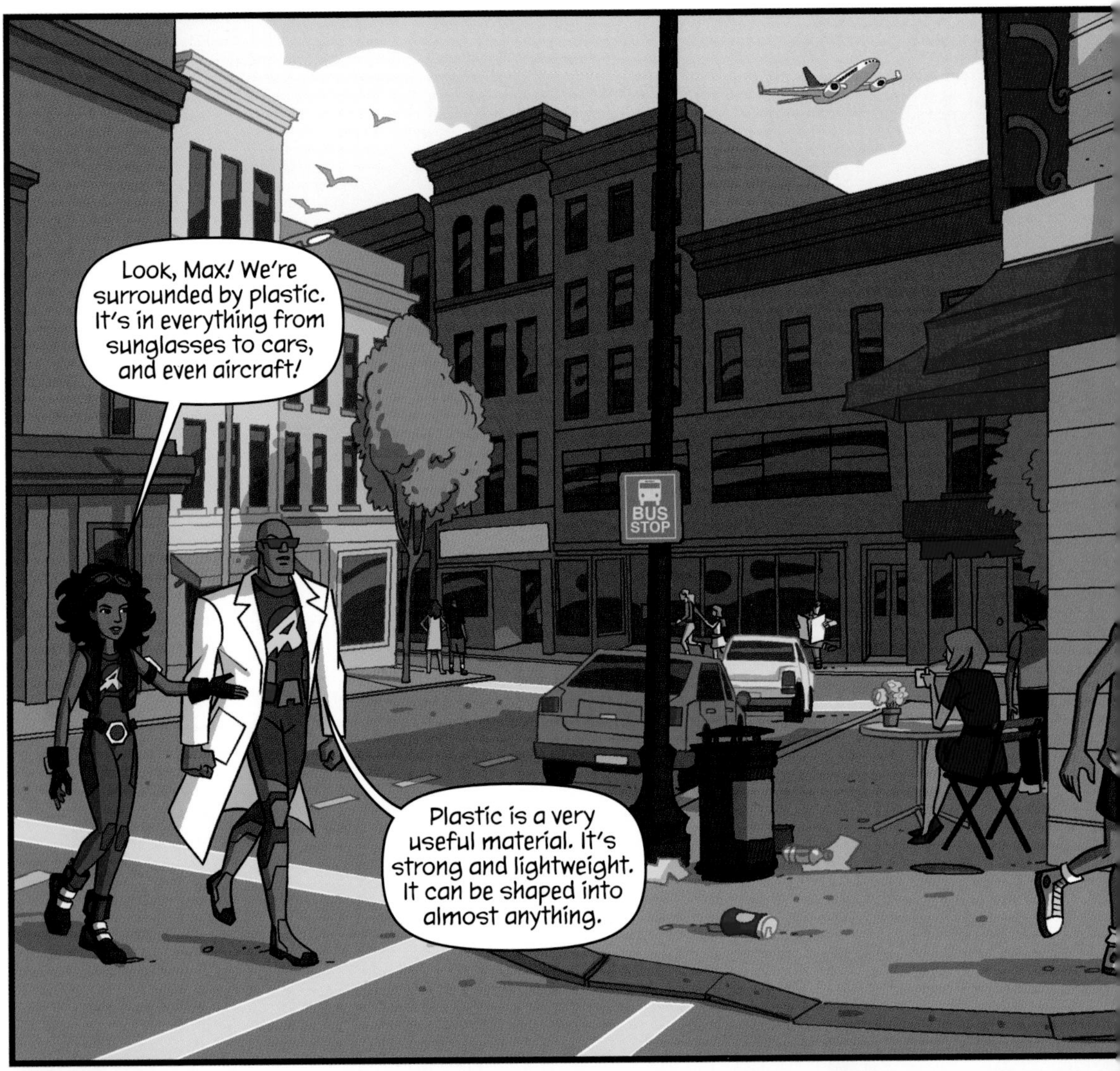
Look, Max! We're surrounded by plastic. It's in everything from sunglasses to cars, and even aircraft!
BUS STOP
Plastic is a very useful material. It's strong and lightweight. It can be shaped into almost anything.

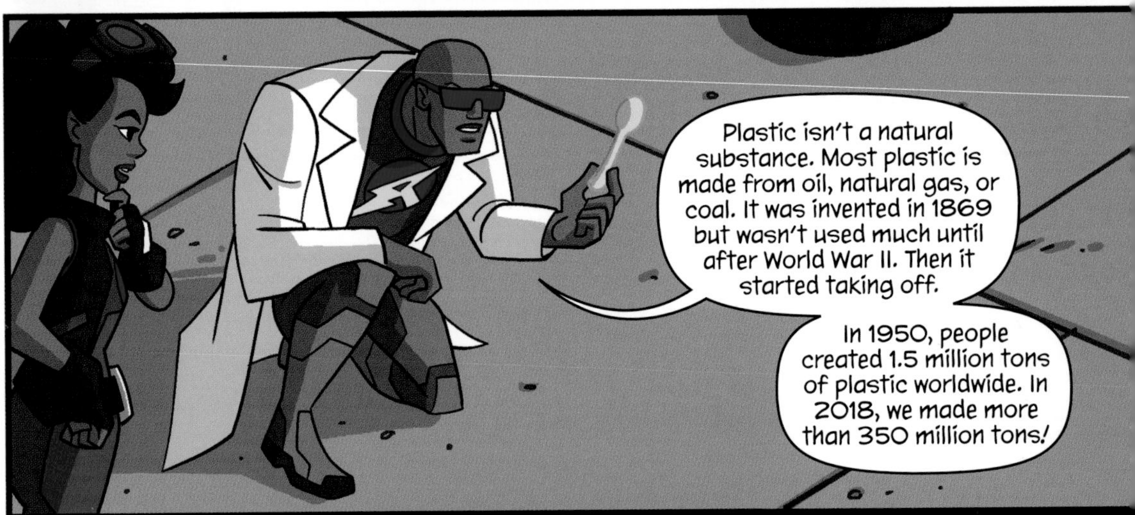
Plastic isn't a natural substance. Most plastic is made from oil, natural gas, or coal. It was invented in 1869 but wasn't used much until after World War II. Then it started taking off.
In 1950, people created 1.5 million tons of plastic worldwide. In 2018, we made more than 350 million tons!

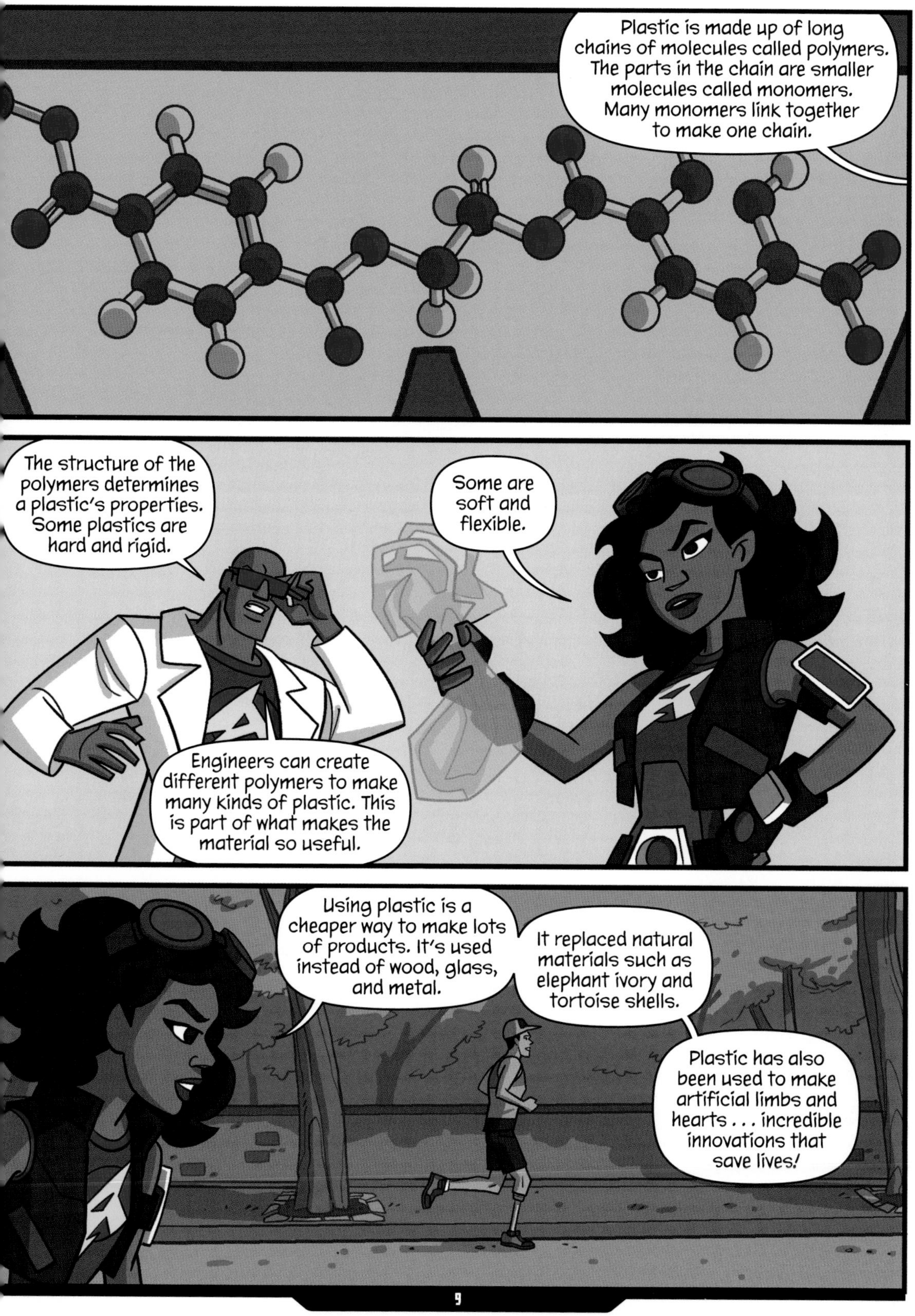
Plastic is made up of long chains of molecules called polymers. The parts in the chain are smaller molecules called monomers. Many monomers link together to make one chain.
The structure of the polymers determines a plastic's properties. Some plastics are hard and rigid.
Some are soft and flexible.
Engineers can create different polymers to make many kinds of plastic. This is part of what makes the material so useful.
Using plastic is a cheaper way to make lots of products. It's used instead of wood, glass, and metal.
It replaced natural materials such as elephant ivory and tortoise shells.
Plastic has also been used to make artificial limbs and hearts . . . incredible innovations that save lives!

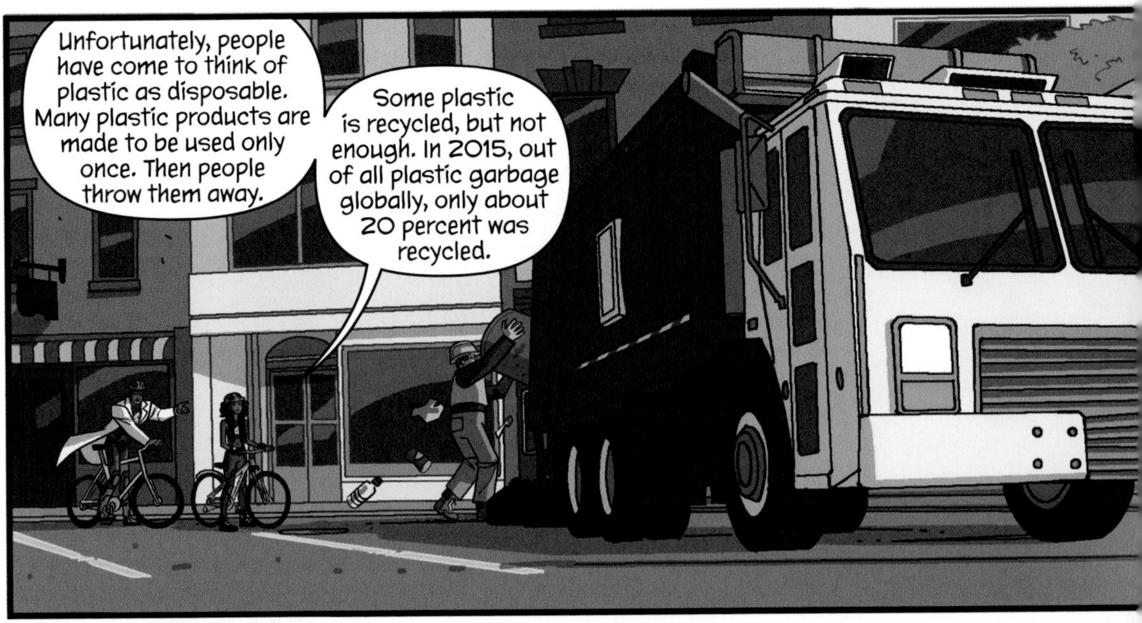
Unfortunately, people have come to think of plastic as disposable. Many plastic products are made to be used only once. Then people throw them away.
Some plastic is recycled, but not enough. In 2015, out of all plastic garbage globally, only about 20 percent was recycled.

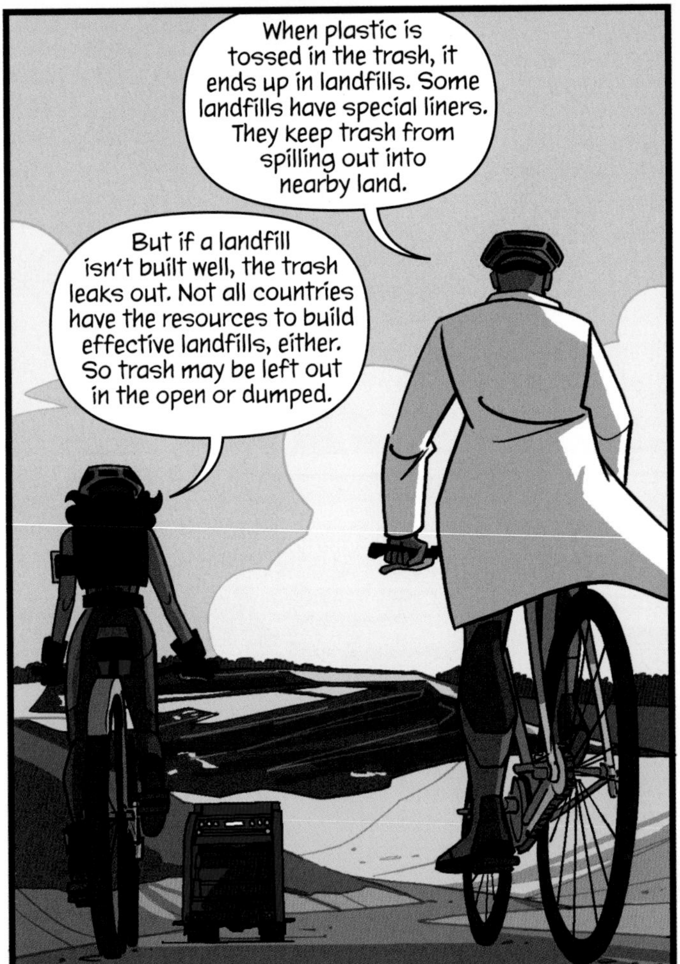
When plastic is tossed in the trash, it ends up in landfills. Some landfills have special liners. They keep trash from spilling out into nearby land.
But if a landfill isn't built well, the trash leaks out. Not all countries have the resources to build effective landfills, either. So trash may be left out in the open or dumped.

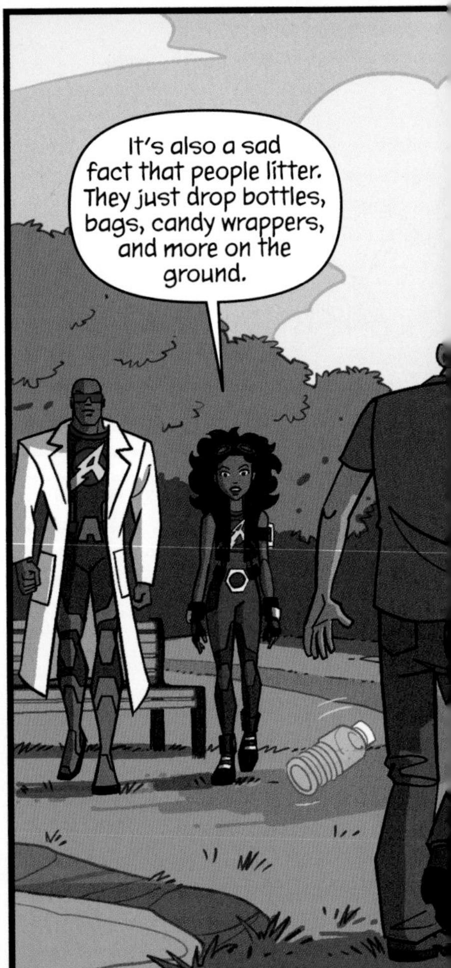
It's also a sad fact that people litter. They just drop bottles, bags, candy wrappers, and more on the ground.

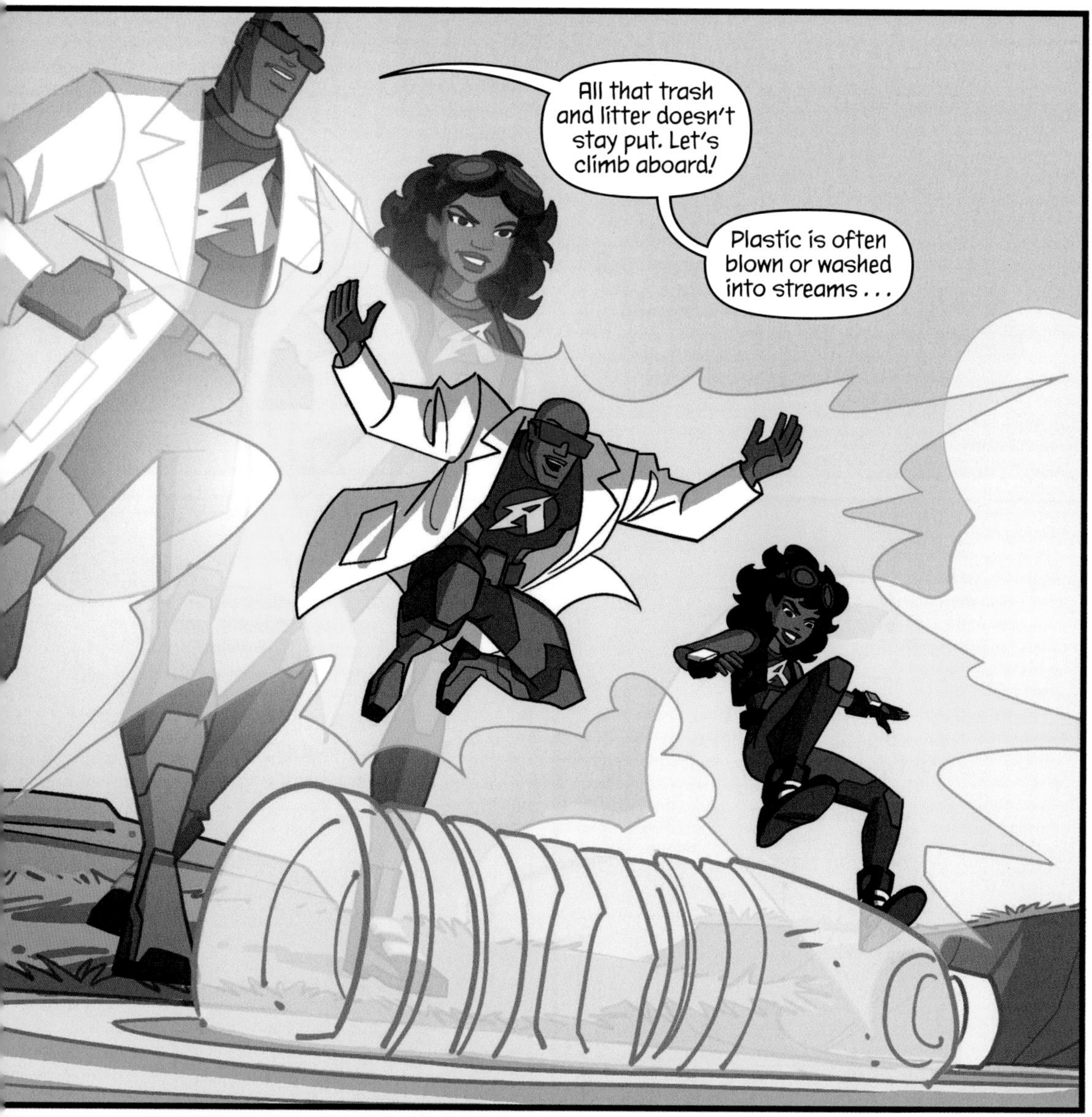
All that trash and litter doesn't stay put. Let's climb aboard!
Plastic is often blown or washed into streams . . .

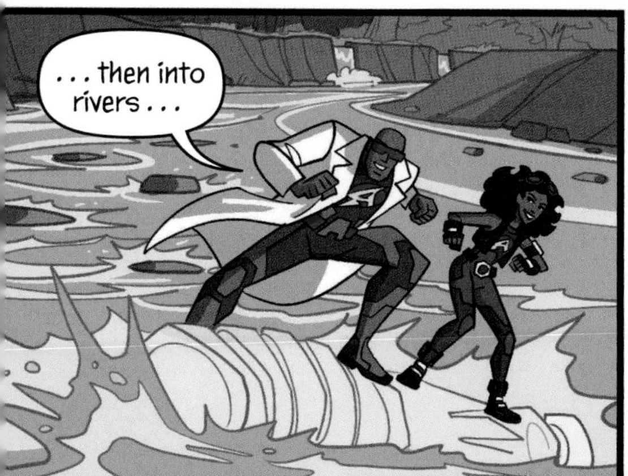
. . . then into rivers . . .

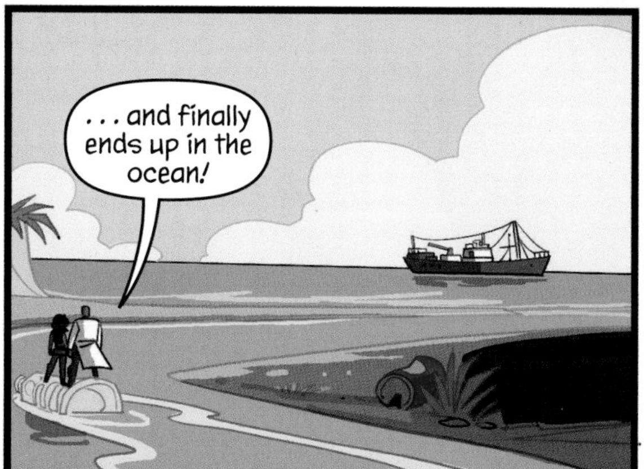
. . . and finally ends up in the ocean!

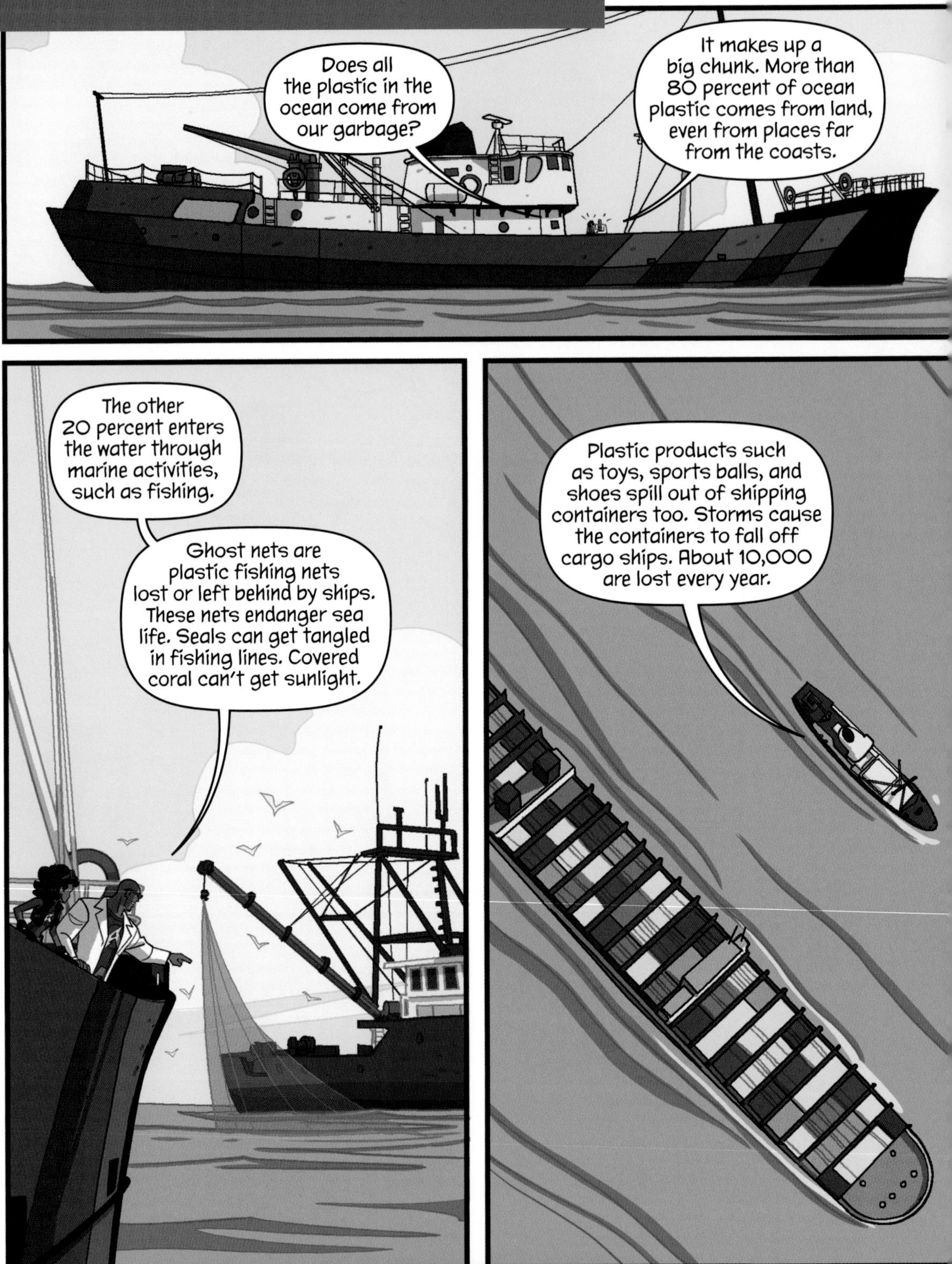
Does all the plastic in the ocean come from our garbage?
It makes up a big chunk. More than 80 percent of ocean plastic comes from land, even from places far from the coasts.
The other 20 percent enters the water through marine activities, such as fishing.
Ghost nets are plastic fishing nets lost or left behind by ships. These nets endanger sea life. Seals can get tangled in fishing lines. Covered coral can't get sunlight.
Plastic products such as toys, sports balls, and shoes spill out of shipping containers too. Storms cause the containers to fall off cargo ships. About 10,000 are lost every year.

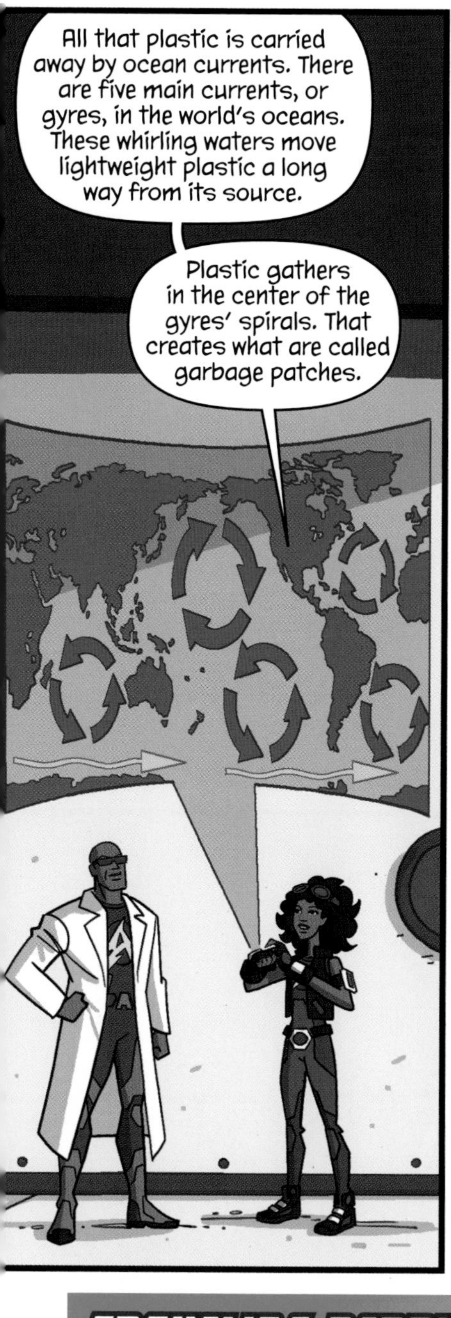
All that plastic is carried away by ocean currents. There are five main currents, or gyres, in the world's oceans. These whirling waters move lightweight plastic a long way from its source.
Plastic gathers in the center of the gyres' spirals. That creates what are called garbage patches.

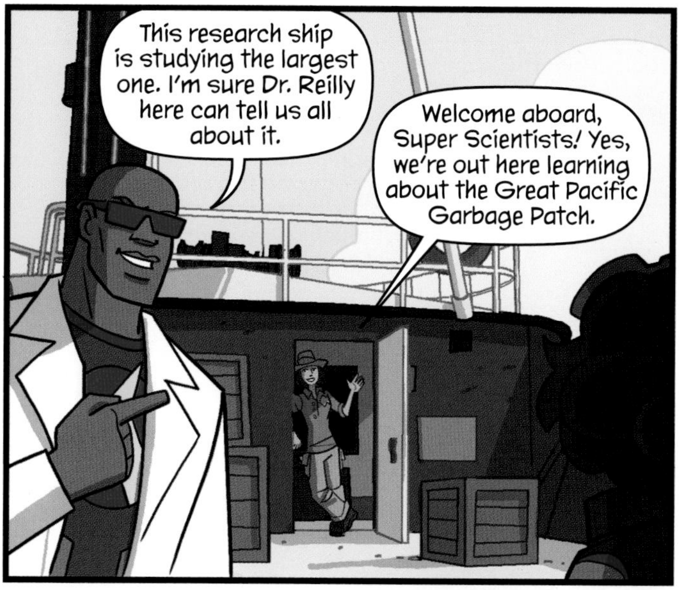
This research ship is studying the largest one. I'm sure Dr. Reilly here can tell us all about it.
Welcome aboard, Super Scientists! Yes, we're out here learning about the Great Pacific Garbage Patch.

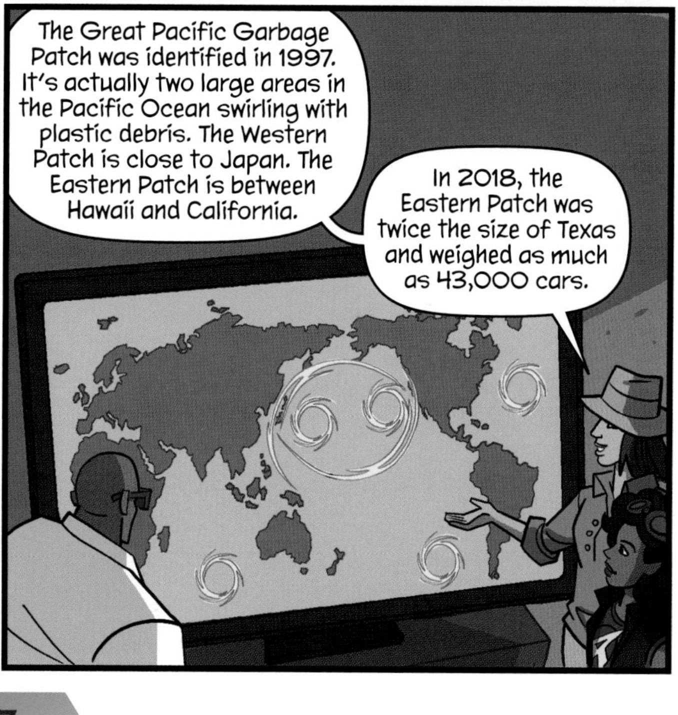
The Great Pacific Garbage Patch was identified in 1997. It's actually two large areas in the Pacific Ocean swirling with plastic debris. The Western Patch is close to Japan. The Eastern Patch is between Hawaii and California.
In 2018, the Eastern Patch was twice the size of Texas and weighed as much as 43,000 cars.

TRAVELING DEBRIS

On March 11, 2011, a 9.0 magnitude earthquake struck off the coast of Japan. A tsunami followed. The disaster killed many people and caused billions of dollars in damage. It also washed an estimated 5 million tons of debris into the Pacific Ocean. Ocean currents carried the plastic debris from the earthquake. The first plastic to reach North America was a soccer ball that washed ashore in Alaska in March 2012.

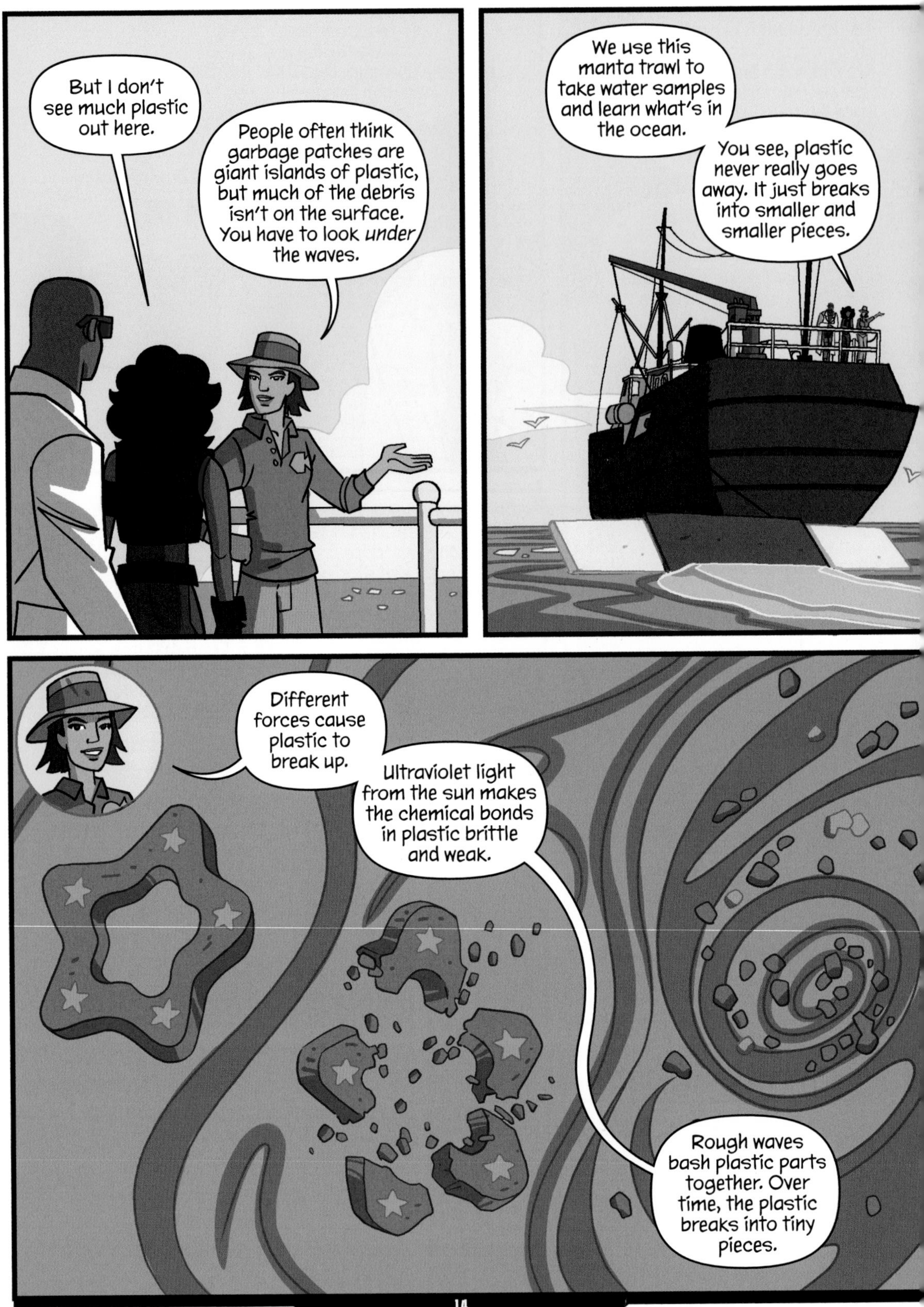

But I don't see much plastic out here.
People often think garbage patches are giant islands of plastic, but much of the debris isn't on the surface. You have to look *under* the waves.
We use this manta trawl to take water samples and learn what's in the ocean.
You see, plastic never really goes away. It just breaks into smaller and smaller pieces.
Different forces cause plastic to break up.
Ultraviolet light from the sun makes the chemical bonds in plastic brittle and weak.
Rough waves bash plastic parts together. Over time, the plastic breaks into tiny pieces.

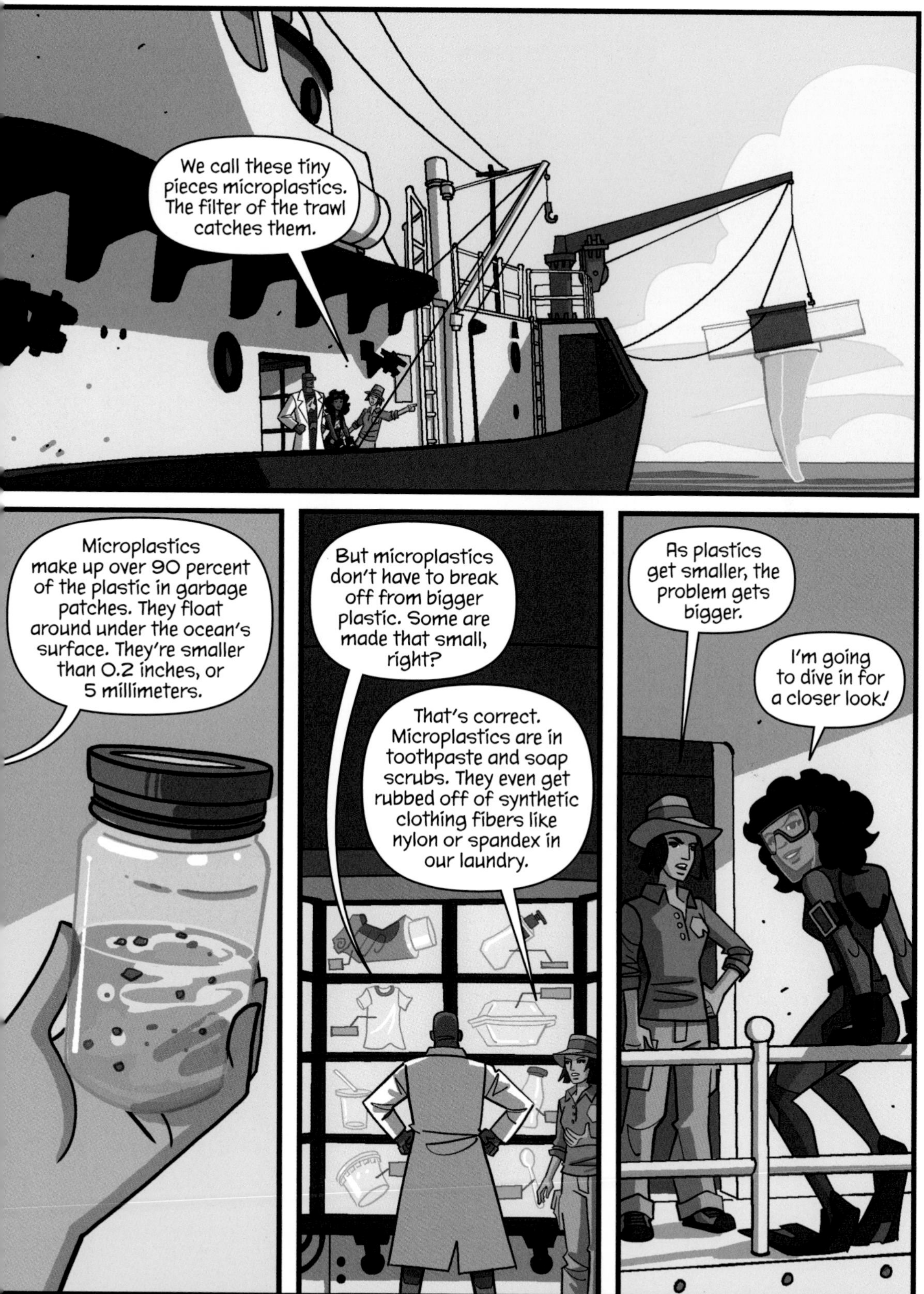
We call these tiny pieces microplastics. The filter of the trawl catches them.
Microplastics make up over 90 percent of the plastic in garbage patches. They float around under the ocean's surface. They're smaller than 0.2 inches, or 5 millimeters.
But microplastics don't have to break off from bigger plastic. Some are made that small, right?
That's correct. Microplastics are in toothpaste and soap scrubs. They even get rubbed off of synthetic clothing fibers like nylon or spandex in our laundry.
As plastics get smaller, the problem gets bigger.
I'm going to dive in for a closer look!

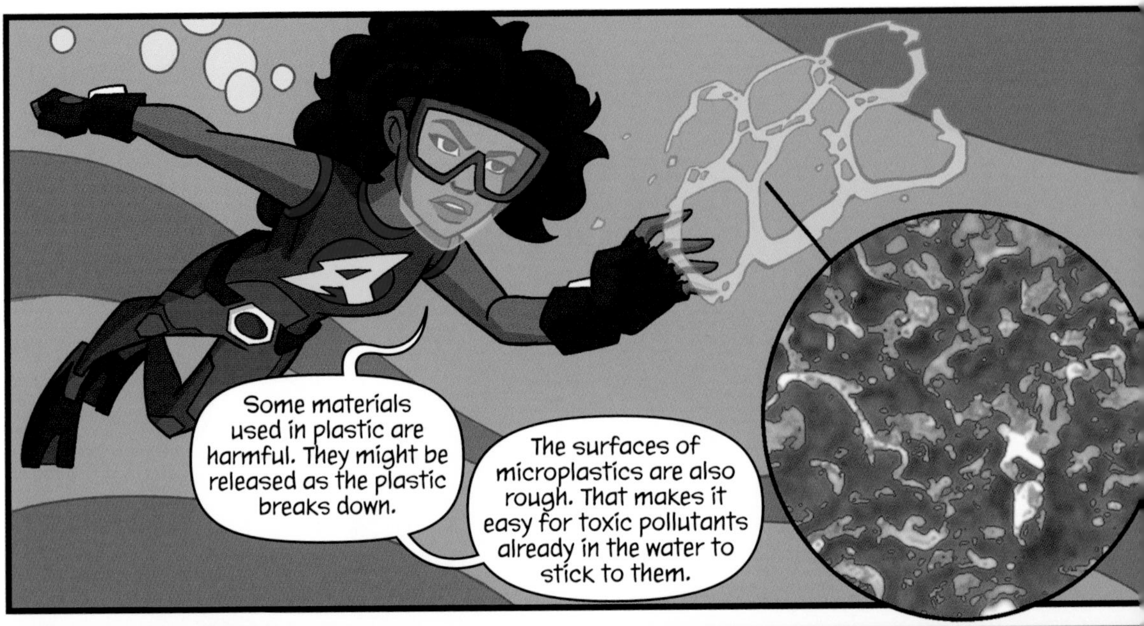
Some materials used in plastic are harmful. They might be released as the plastic breaks down.
The surfaces of microplastics are also rough. That makes it easy for toxic pollutants already in the water to stick to them.

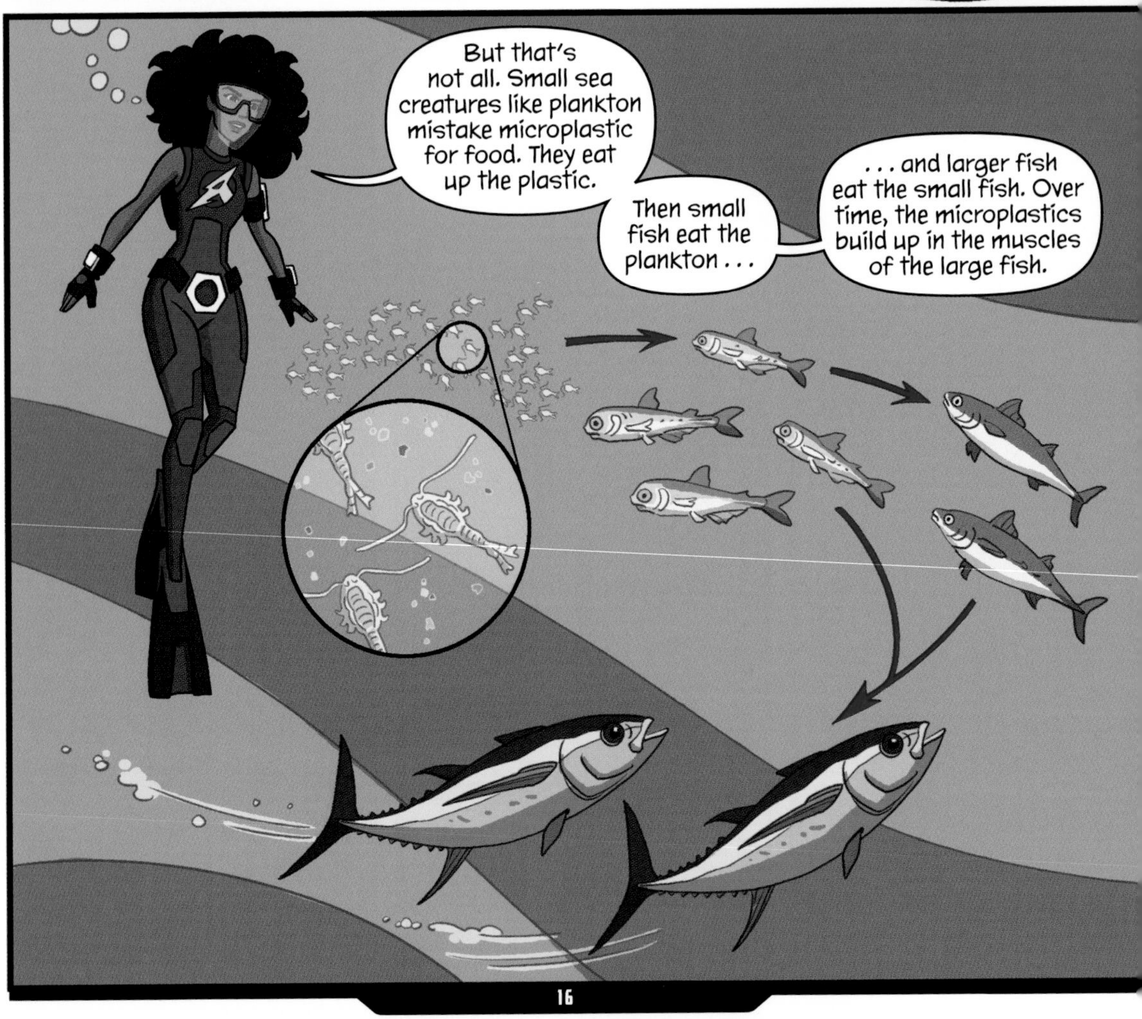
But that's not all. Small sea creatures like plankton mistake microplastic for food. They eat up the plastic.
Then small fish eat the plankton . . .
. . . and larger fish eat the small fish. Over time, the microplastics build up in the muscles of the large fish.

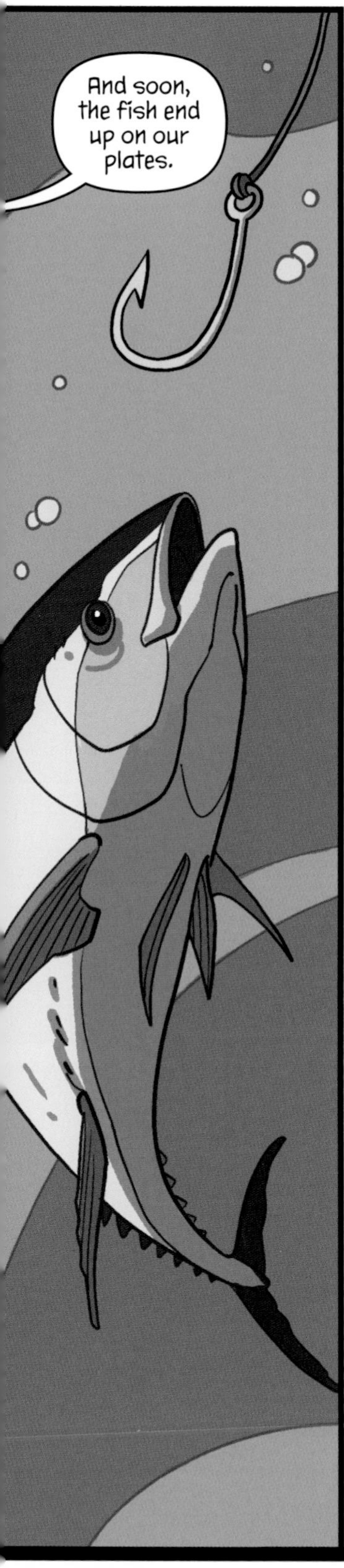
And soon, the fish end up on our plates.

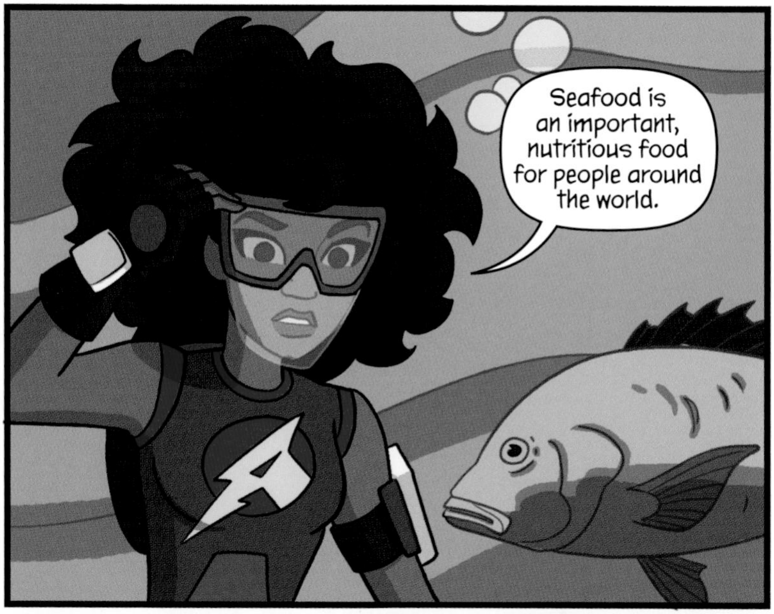
Seafood is an important, nutritious food for people around the world.

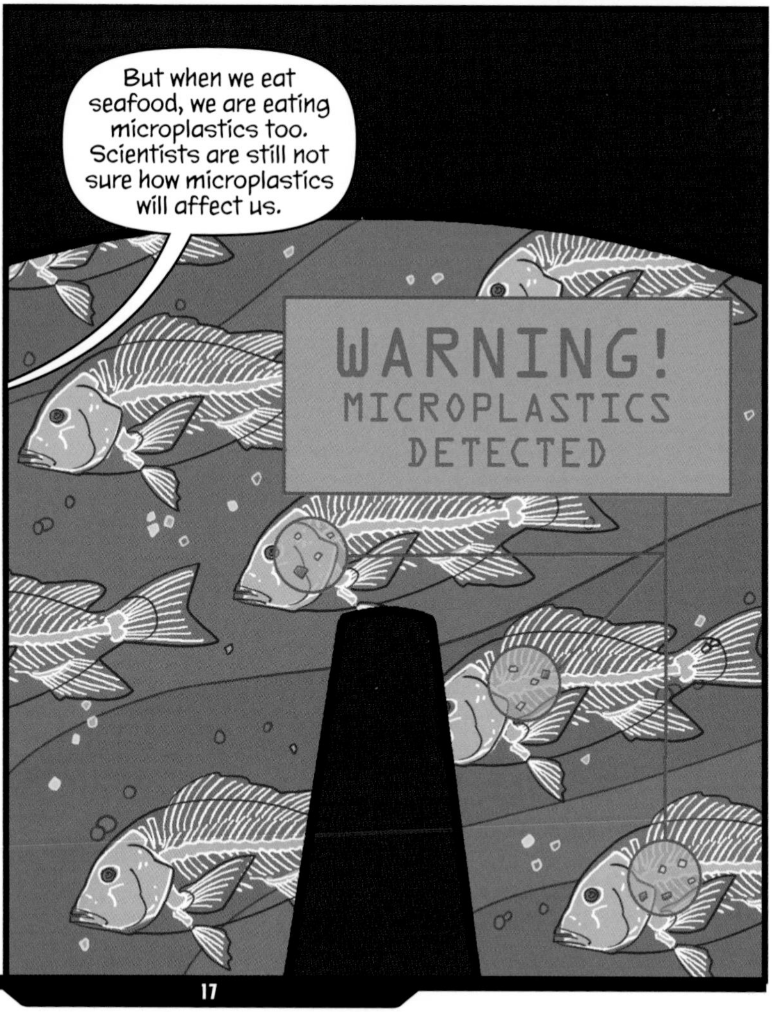
But when we eat seafood, we are eating microplastics too. Scientists are still not sure how microplastics will affect us.
WARNING!
MICROPLASTICS
DETECTED

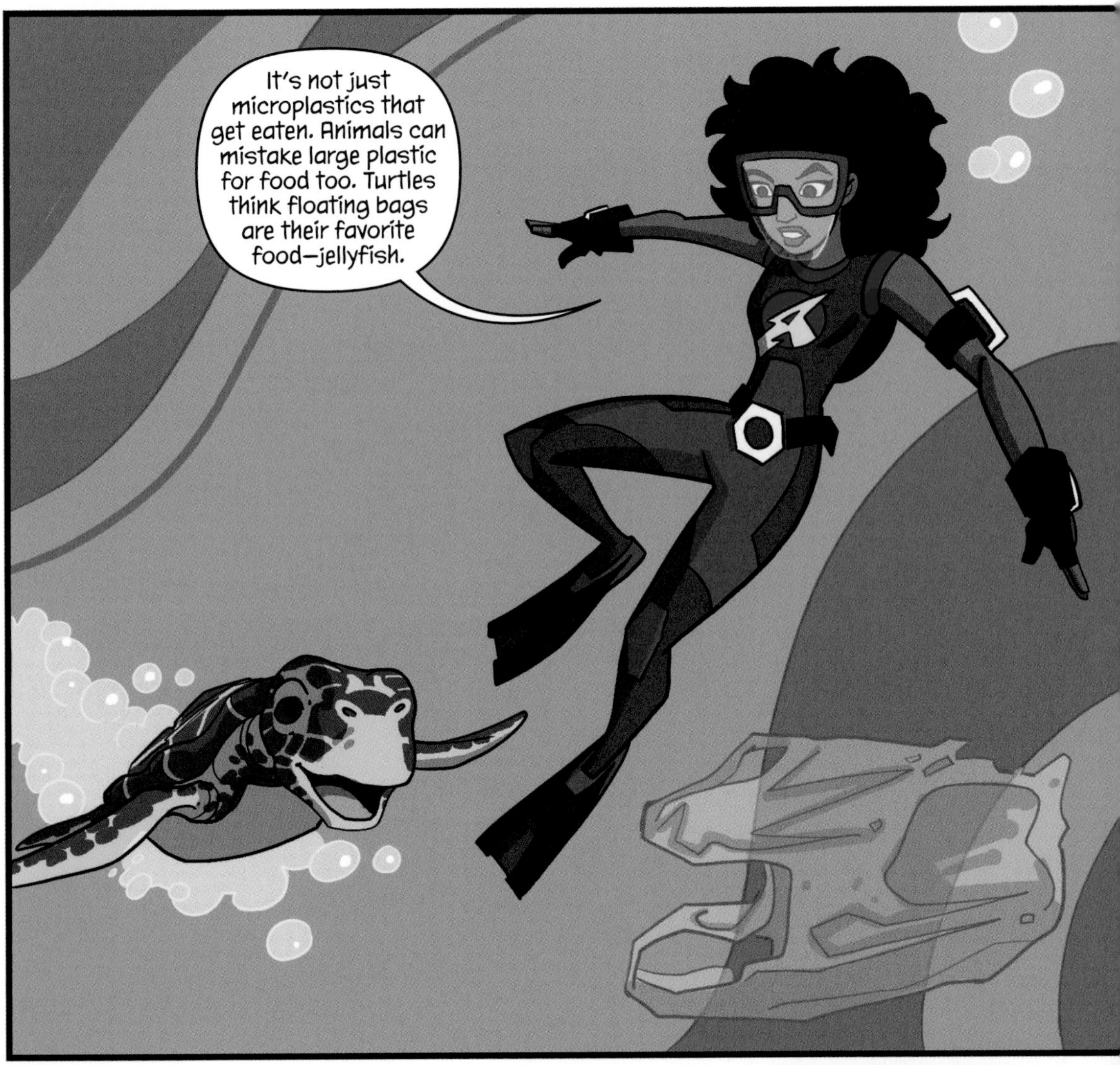
It's not just microplastics that get eaten. Animals can mistake large plastic for food too. Turtles think floating bags are their favorite food—jellyfish.

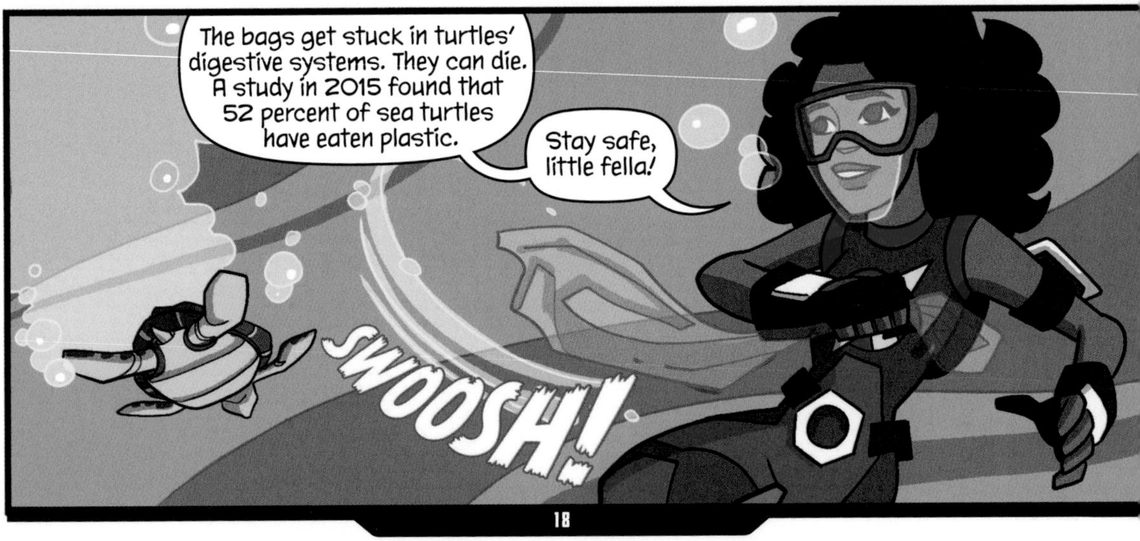
The bags get stuck in turtles' digestive systems. They can die. A study in 2015 found that 52 percent of sea turtles have eaten plastic.
Stay safe, little fella!
SWOOSH!

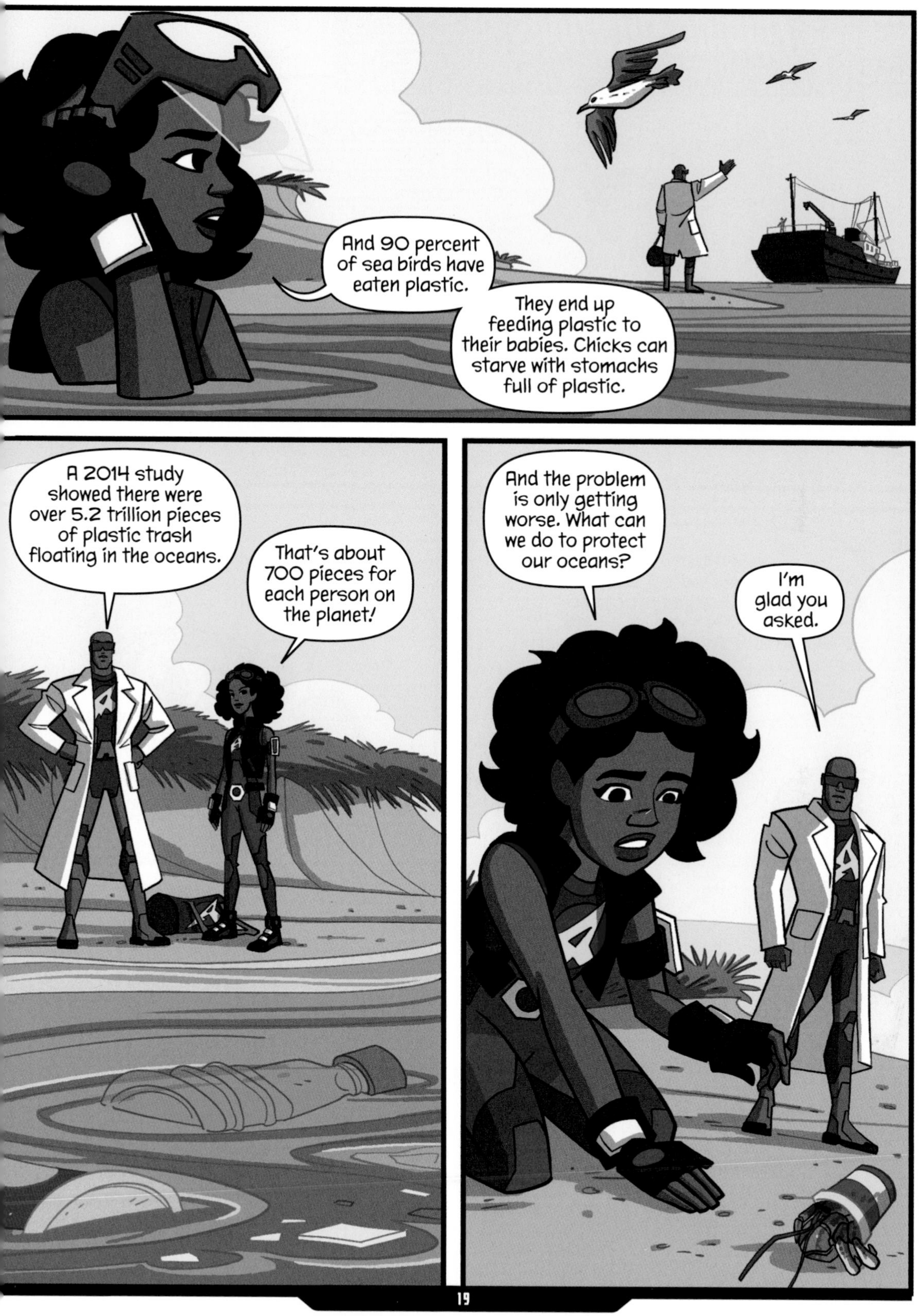

And 90 percent of sea birds have eaten plastic.
They end up feeding plastic to their babies. Chicks can starve with stomachs full of plastic.
A 2014 study showed there were over 5.2 trillion pieces of plastic trash floating in the oceans.
That's about 700 pieces for each person on the planet!
And the problem is only getting worse. What can we do to protect our oceans?
I'm glad you asked.

Many people are looking for unique solutions to our plastic problem.

Dutch entrepreneur Boyan Slat was only 18 when he started The Ocean Cleanup.

The group invented a net-like device to catch floating plastic. It gets carried through the ocean by waves and wind. As it moves, a large U-shaped tube gathers plastic on the surface. Screens hang down to catch plastic in the water.

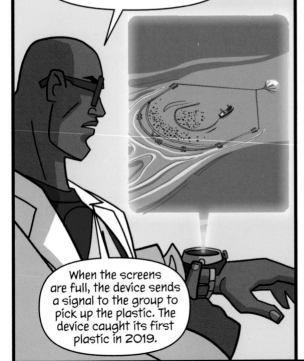

When the screens are full, the device sends a signal to the group to pick up the plastic. The device caught its first plastic in 2019.

The Ocean Cleanup and other groups have also invented systems that catch plastic in rivers before it enters the ocean.

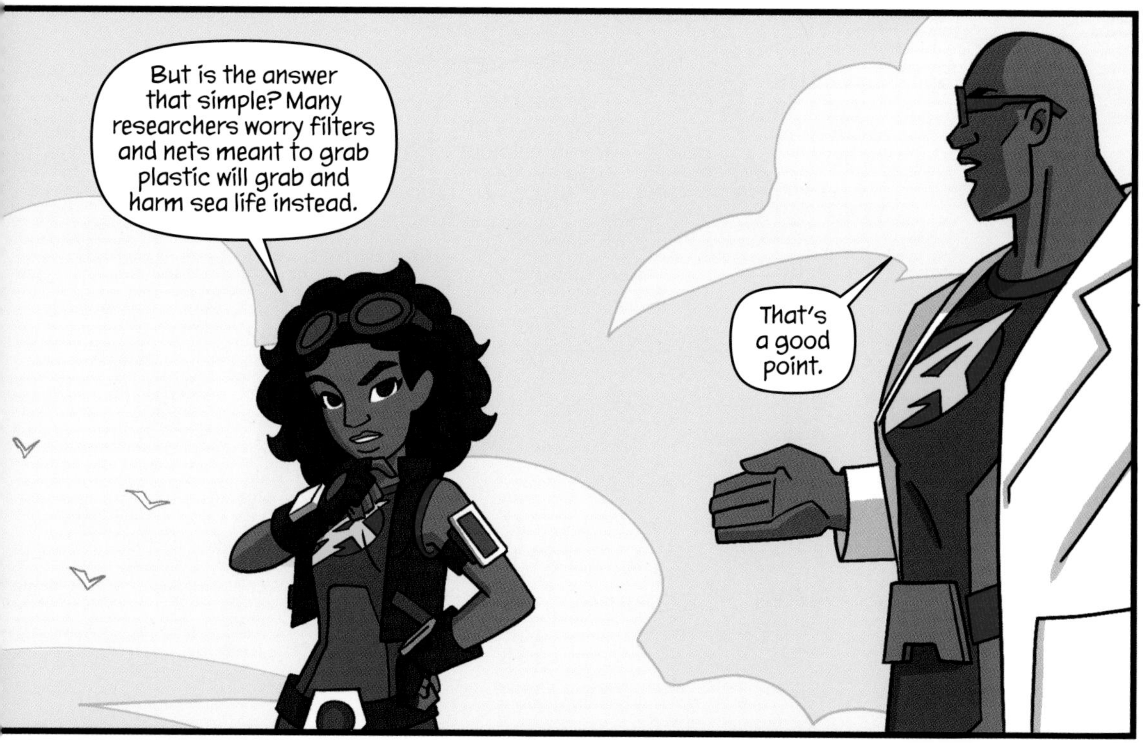
But is the answer that simple? Many researchers worry filters and nets meant to grab plastic will grab and harm sea life instead.
That's a good point.

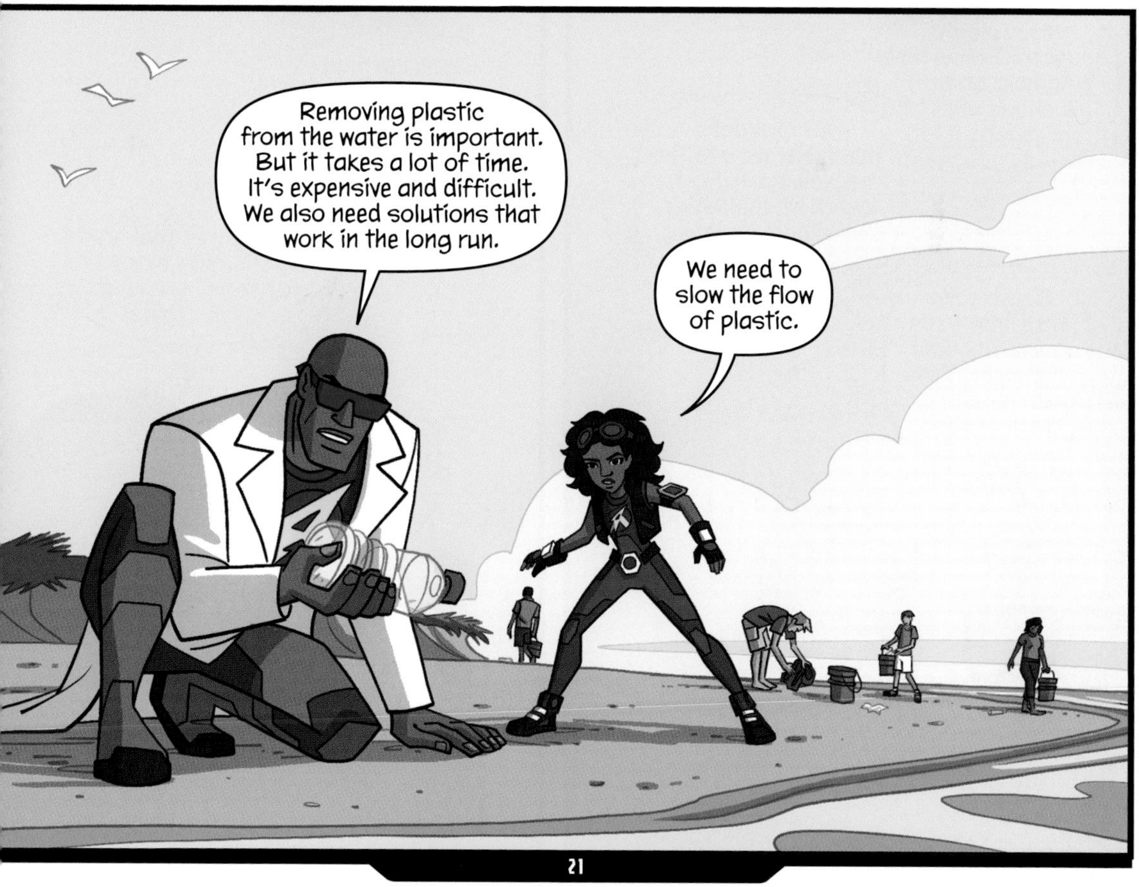
Removing plastic from the water is important. But it takes a lot of time. It's expensive and difficult. We also need solutions that work in the long run.
We need to slow the flow of plastic.

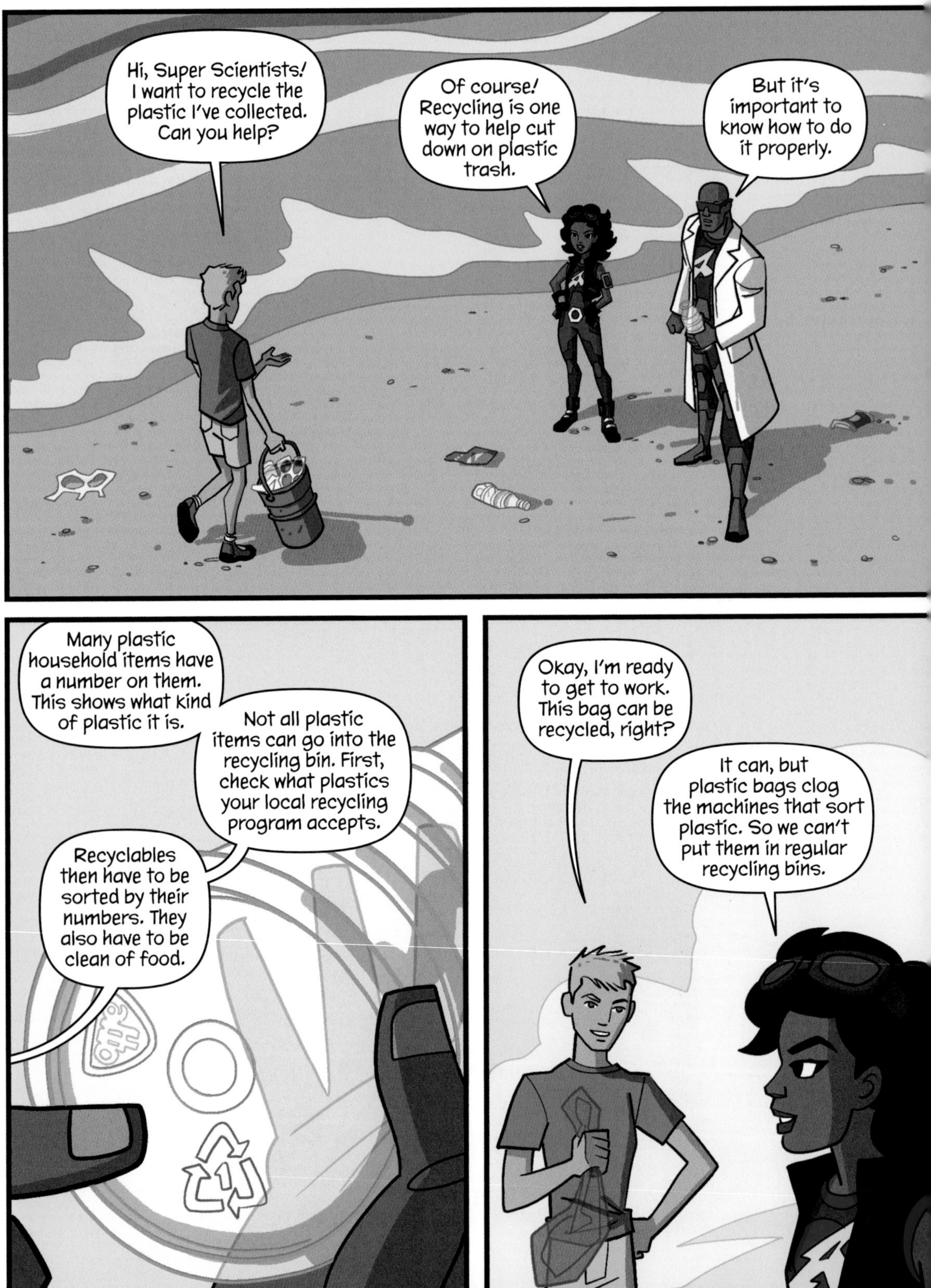
Hi, Super Scientists! I want to recycle the plastic I've collected. Can you help?
Of course! Recycling is one way to help cut down on plastic trash.
But it's important to know how to do it properly.
Many plastic household items have a number on them. This shows what kind of plastic it is.
Not all plastic items can go into the recycling bin. First, check what plastics your local recycling program accepts.
Recyclables then have to be sorted by their numbers. They also have to be clean of food.
Okay, I'm ready to get to work. This bag can be recycled, right?
It can, but plastic bags clog the machines that sort plastic. So we can't put them in regular recycling bins.

What about these?
The bottle is recyclable. But not the cap. Styrofoam can't be recycled either.
Hmm, I'll get the hang of it. Thanks for your help!
Recycling is worth it, but it is kind of complicated. I can see why people get frustrated and give up on it.
And if a community, or an entire country, doesn't have recycling programs, even recyclable plastic just ends up in the trash.
Recycling is only part of the solution to ending ocean plastics.

PLASTIC TYPES

Not all plastic is recyclable. There are two main types of plastic: thermoset and thermoplastic. "Thermo" means heat. Thermoplastics can be melted and made into new products. Plastic bottles are thermoplastics. But thermoset plastics can't be recycled. Their polymer bonds won't change with heat. Plastic table tops and Formula 1 race cars are made from thermoset plastics.

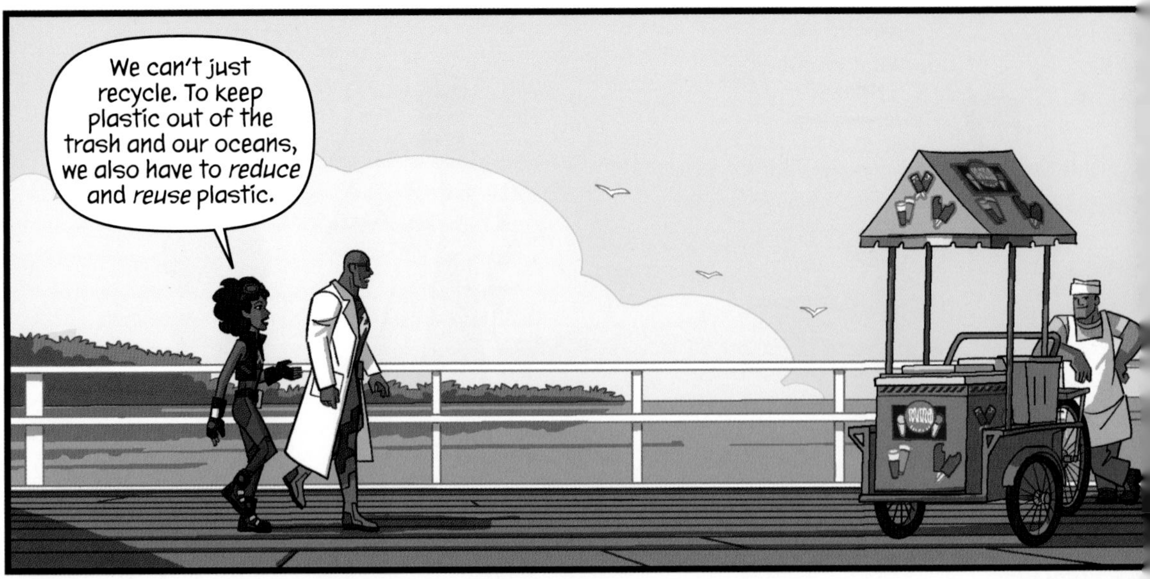
We can't just recycle. To keep plastic out of the trash and our oceans, we also have to *reduce* and *reuse* plastic.

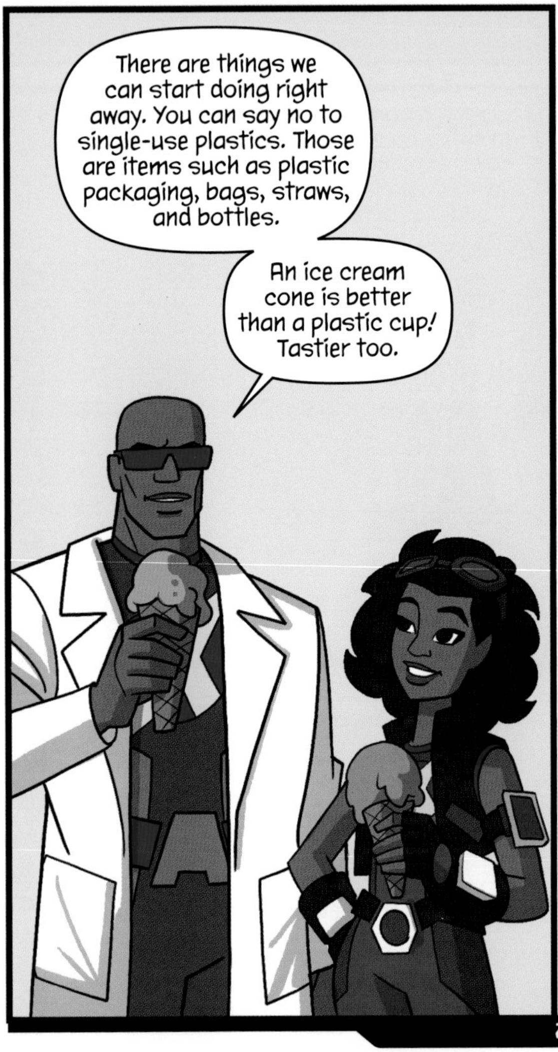
There are things we can start doing right away. You can say no to single-use plastics. Those are items such as plastic packaging, bags, straws, and bottles.
An ice cream cone is better than a plastic cup! Tastier too.

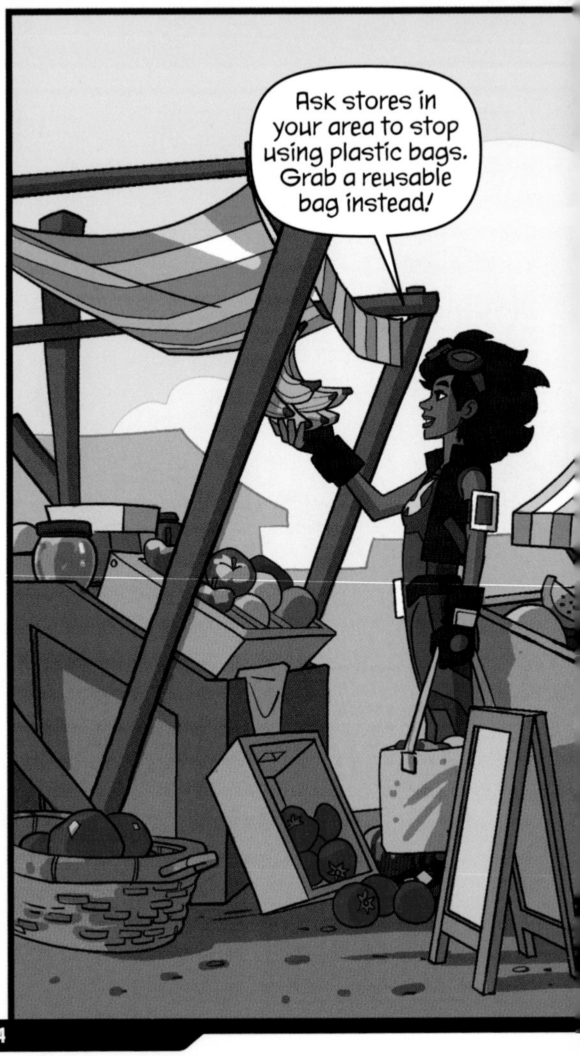
Ask stores in your area to stop using plastic bags. Grab a reusable bag instead!

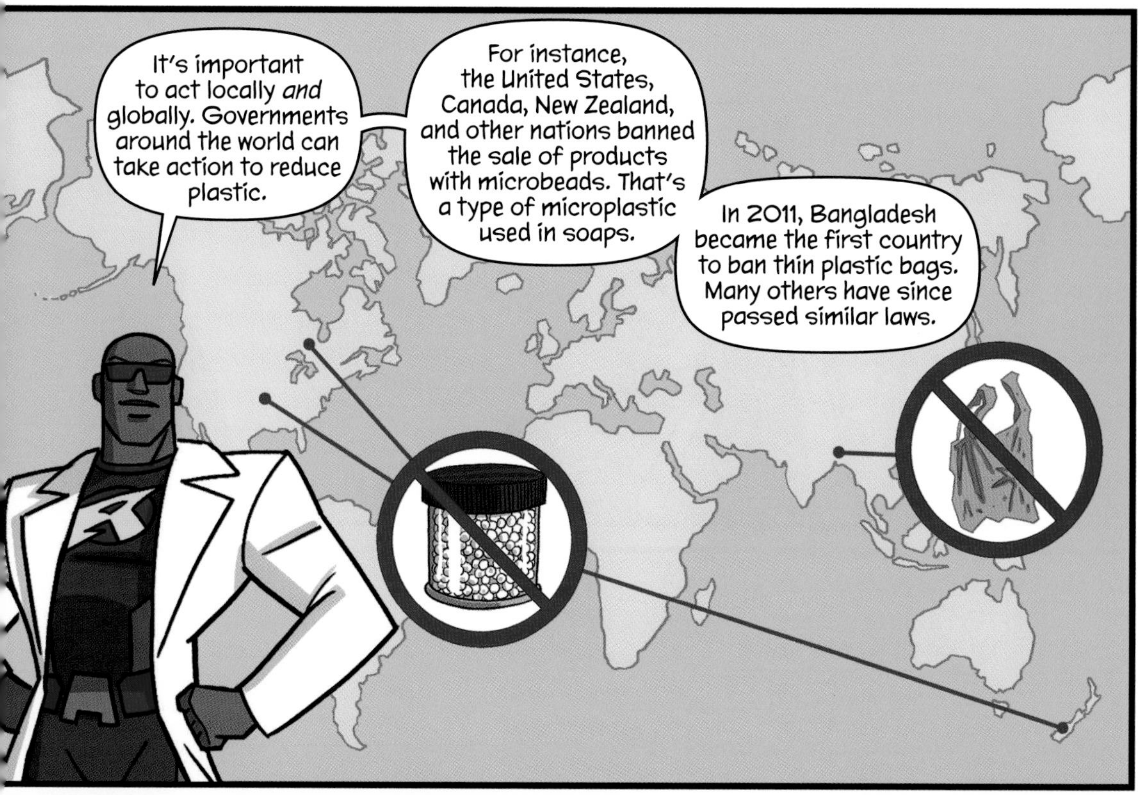
It's important to act locally *and* globally. Governments around the world can take action to reduce plastic.
For instance, the United States, Canada, New Zealand, and other nations banned the sale of products with microbeads. That's a type of microplastic used in soaps.
In 2011, Bangladesh became the first country to ban thin plastic bags. Many others have since passed similar laws.

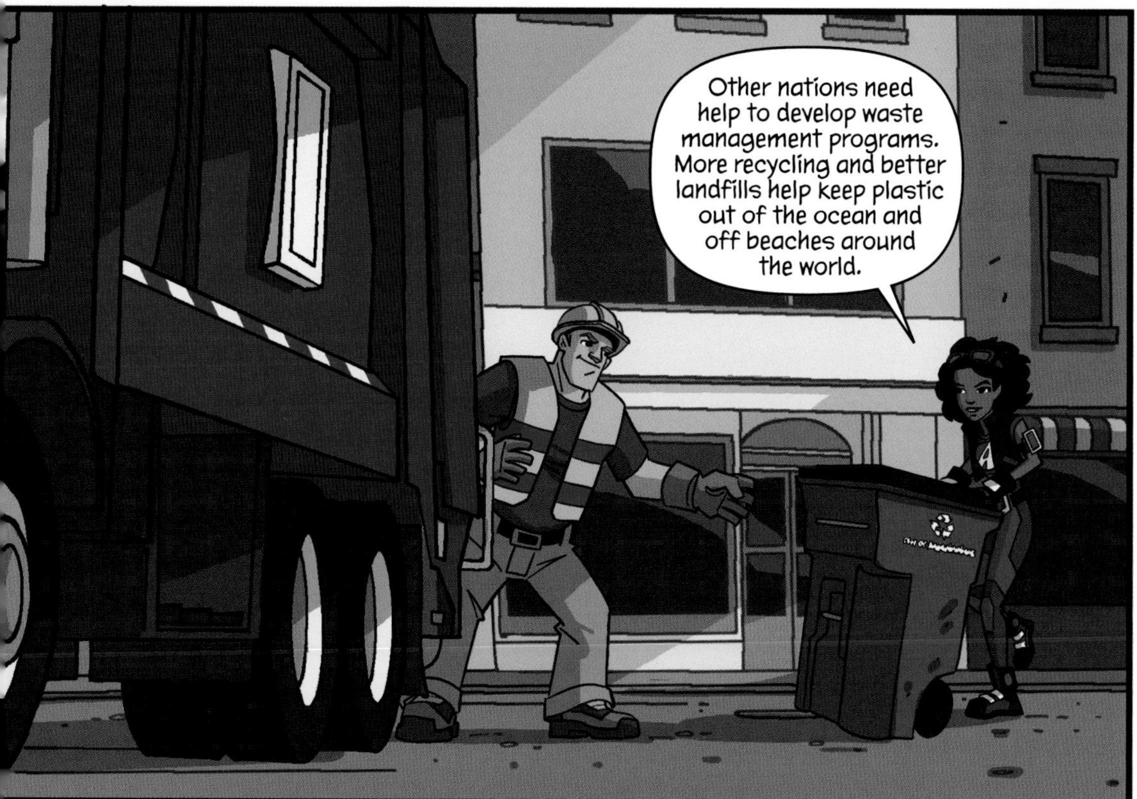
Other nations need help to develop waste management programs. More recycling and better landfills help keep plastic out of the ocean and off beaches around the world.

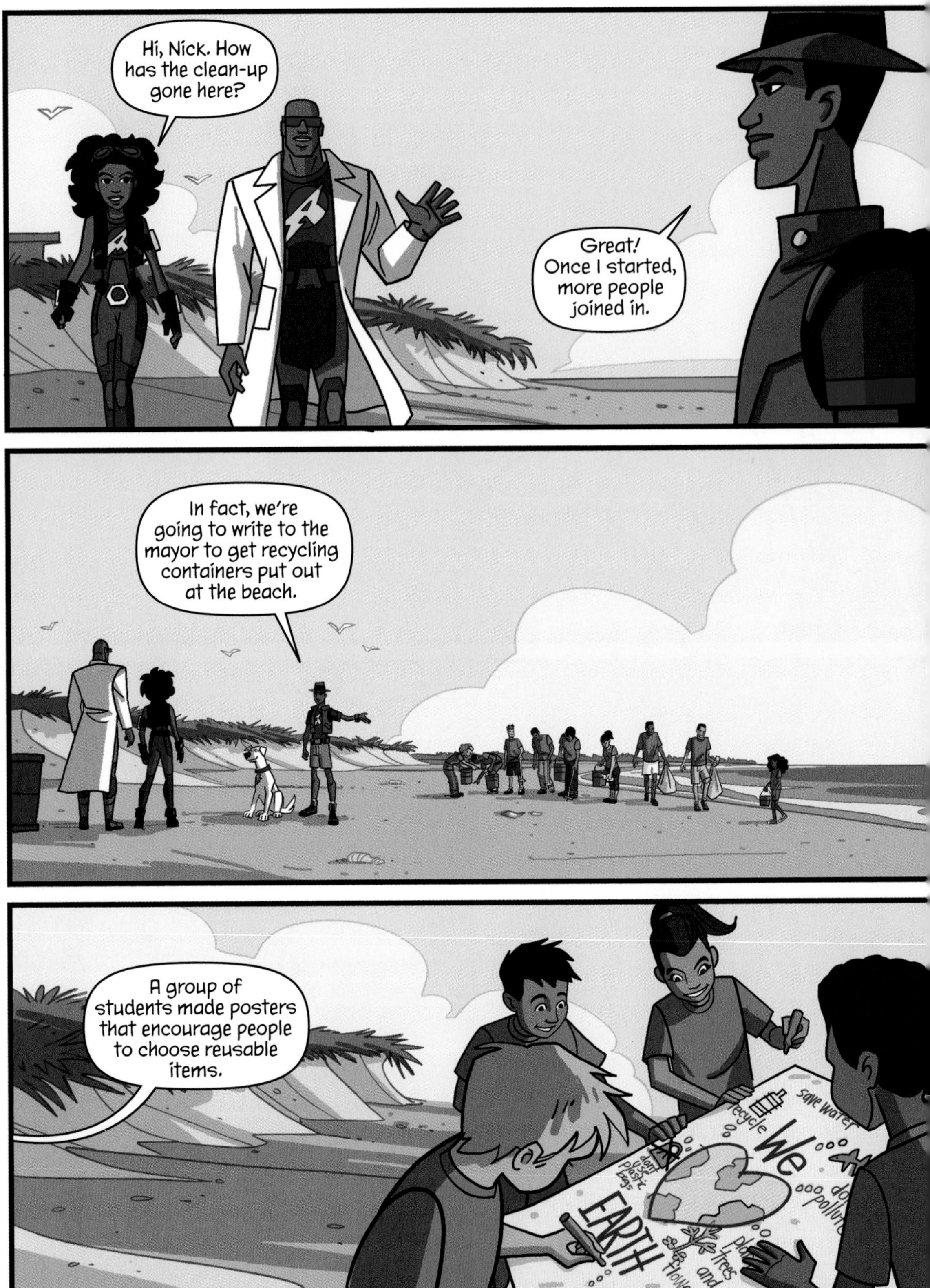
Hi, Nick. How has the clean-up gone here?
Great! Once I started, more people joined in.
In fact, we're going to write to the mayor to get recycling containers put out at the beach.
A group of students made posters that encourage people to choose reusable items.
save water
recycle
We
EARTH
trees
and
flowers

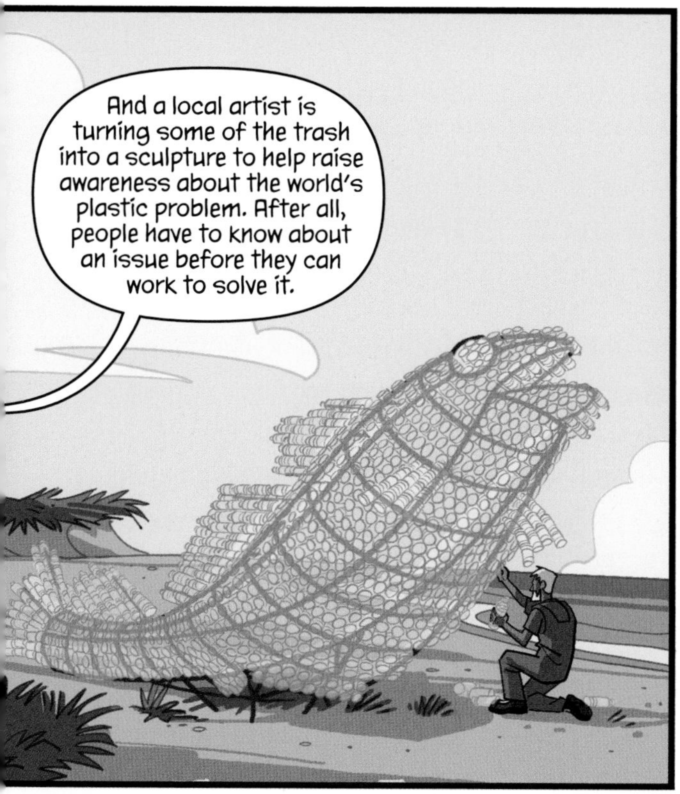
And a local artist is turning some of the trash into a sculpture to help raise awareness about the world's plastic problem. After all, people have to know about an issue before they can work to solve it.

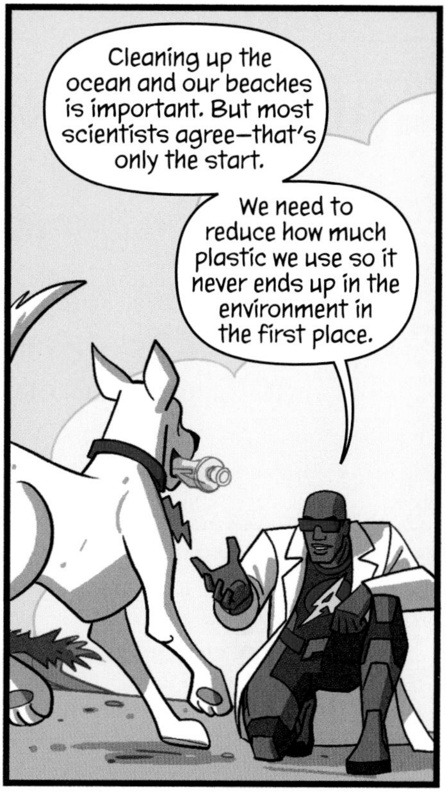
Cleaning up the ocean and our beaches is important. But most scientists agree—that's only the start.
We need to reduce how much plastic we use so it never ends up in the environment in the first place.

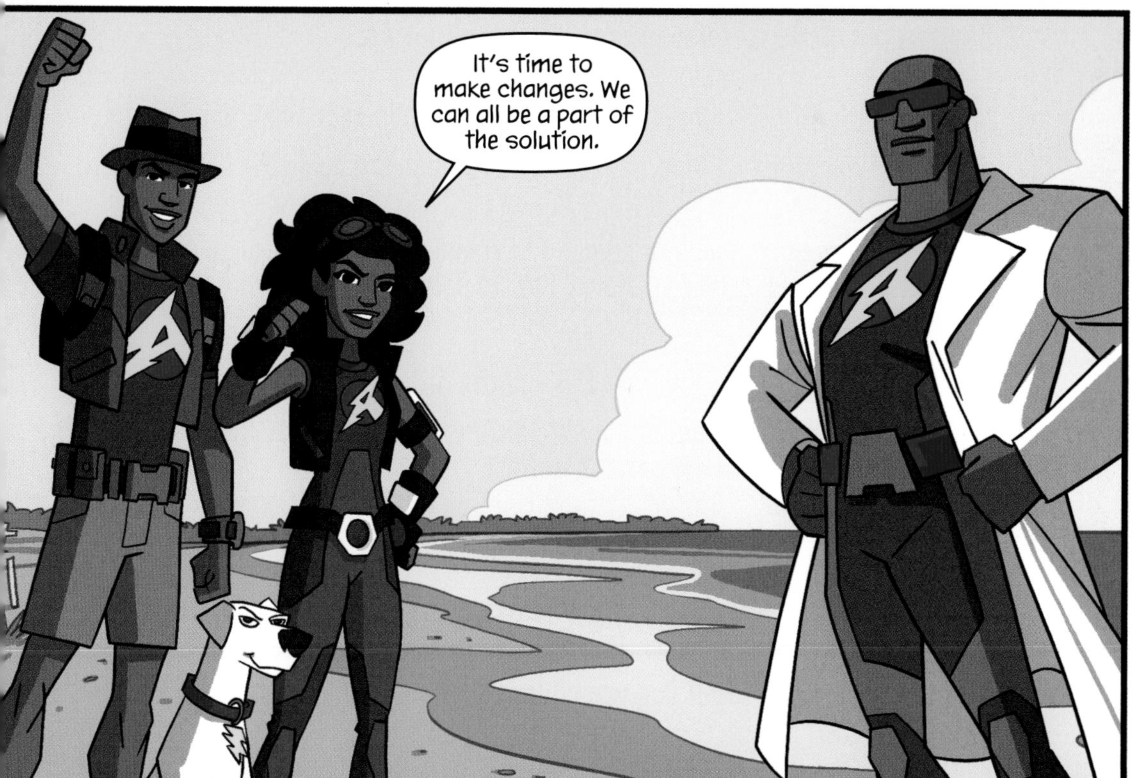
It's time to make changes. We can all be a part of the solution.

TAKE ACTION!

Reducing plastic is a worldwide project. But you can start working on it now in your neighborhood.

- Plan ahead! Keep a reusable water bottle with you, have a set of utensils handy for on-the-go meals, and carry a reusable shopping bag.

- Don't trash plastic furniture or utensils. Donate them to a charity or a program like the Freecycle Network so others can use items you don't need anymore.

- Reuse plastic items for as long as you can. Clean plastic takeout containers and reuse them in your lunch. Grow plants in a plastic juice jug. Then water them with a watering can made from a clean plastic laundry detergent bottle.

- Get creative! Think of new uses for plastic items. Find out what plastics your town recycles. Make sure you always recycle those items.

- Write to your local government and ask them to help increase recycling in your schools and community. Encourage friends and neighbors to do the same.

- Start a poster campaign in your school or neighborhood. Teach people about why it's important to reduce, reuse, and recycle plastics.

- Pick up plastic in your neighborhood. If you can recycle it, do it! If not, cleaning up litter keeps it out of our streams, rivers, and oceans.

- When you are shopping, try to pick products with no packaging or recyclable packaging. If you can, shop at a farmer's market or community market. Buying local usually means less plastic packages.

- Try a plastic-free challenge! Can you go through a day without using plastic?

MORE PLASTIC FACTS

Some scientists think the plastic trash floating near the surface is only 1 percent of all the plastic in the ocean. It is also building up on the ocean floor. Recent studies discovered that there is more plastic on the ocean floor than is floating near the surface. The deepest piece of plastic was found in the Marianas Trench in 2018 at 36,000 feet (11 kilometers) deep!

Plastic is found around the world—even in places where humans don't live! Microplastics have been found in the snow in Antarctica. On uninhabited islands such as Milman Island near Australia, plastic is ruining what should be beautiful beaches. Sea turtle researchers collected more than 165 pounds (75 kg) of plastic from the shore.

Scientists and businesses are working on creative alternatives to plastics. One company in London is developing a plastic made from seaweed. This plastic is not only biodegradable—it's edible!

Scientists in Korea may have discovered a beetle larvae that can eat, digest, and break down a specific kind of plastic called polystyrene.

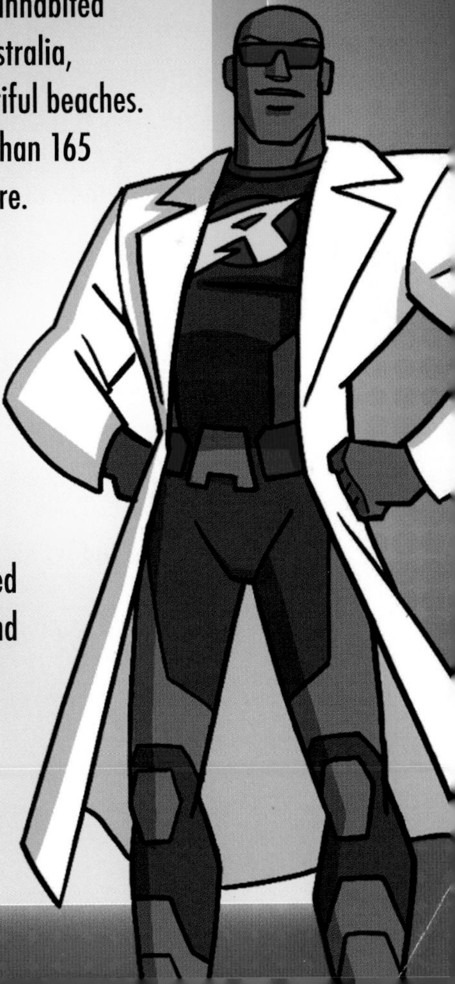

GLOSSARY

disposable (dih-SPOH-zuh-buhl)—made to be thrown away

gyre (JAHYUR)—a large system of rotating ocean currents

landfill (LAND-fil)—a place where garbage is buried

litter (LIH-tuhr)—trash that has been thrown on the ground or carelessly left somewhere

manta trawl (MAN-tuh TRAWL)—a netted device that is pulled through water to collect water samples

microplastic (mye-kroh-PLAS-tik)—a piece of plastic less than 0.2 inches (5 mm); microplastics can be made to be of small size or they are pieces that break off from large plastic

monomer (MAH-nuh-muhr)—a single molecule that can be linked to other molecules

plastic (PLAS-tik)—a strong, lightweight material created by people that can be formed into many shapes when heated and then set as it cools

pollutant (puh-LOOT-uhnt)—a material that can damage the environment

polymer (PAH-luh-muhr)—a group of many monomers linked together

recycle (ree-SYE-kuhl)—to make used items into new products

reduce (rih-DOOS)—to make something smaller in size or quantity

READ MORE

Howell, Izzi. *Pollution Eco Facts.* New York: Crabtree Publishing Company, 2019.

Hustad, Douglas. *Cleaning Up Plastic with Artificial Coastlines.* Minneapolis: Abdo Publishing, 2020.

Smith-Llera, Danielle. *Trash Vortex: How Plastic Pollution Is Choking the World's Oceans.* North Mankato, MN: Compass Point Books, 2018.

INTERNET SITES

National Geographic Kids: Kids vs. Plastic
kids.nationalgeographic.com/explore/nature/kids-vs-plastic/

National Ocean Service: A Guide to Plastic in the Ocean
oceanservice.noaa.gov/hazards/marinedebris/plastics-in-the-ocean.html

TIME for Kids: The Problem with Plastics
timeforkids.com/g34/the-problem-with-plastic/

INDEX

beaches, 7, 25, 26, 27, 29

cleanup efforts, 26–27, 28, 29
  nets and filters, 20–21
creatures at risk, 6, 7, 12, 16, 17,
  18, 19, 21

governments, 25, 28
Great Pacific Garbage Patch, 13

landfills, 10, 25

Marianas Trench, 29

oceans, 7, 11, 12–19, 25, 27, 28, 29

plastic
  alternatives, 29
  garbage, 6, 7, 10–11, 12, 13, 19,
    22, 23, 27, 28, 29
  garbage patches, 13–15
  history of, 8
  ingredients of, 8
  kinds of, 9, 22, 23, 25, 29
  microplastics, 14–18, 25, 29
  products made from, 8, 9, 10,
    12, 15, 22–23, 24, 25, 28
  properties of, 9
  structure of, 9
  polymers, 9, 23

recycling plastics, 10, 22–23, 24, 25,
  26, 28
reducing plastics, 24, 25, 27, 28
reusing plastics, 24, 26, 27, 28
rivers, 11, 20, 28

shipping containers, 12
Slat, Boyan, 20

The Ocean Cleanup, 20
toxic pollution, 16

ultraviolet light, 14